Shelly's SONG

Shelly's SONG

Jim Thornton

SHELLY'S SONG

iUniverse books may be ordered through booksellers or by contacting:

iUniverse
1663 Liberty Drive
Bloomington, IN 47403
www.iuniverse.com
1-800-Authors (1-800-288-4677)

ISBN: 978-1-4917-6540-1 (sc)
ISBN: 978-1-4917-6541-8 (e)

Library of Congress Control Number: 2015906516

Print information available on the last page.

iUniverse rev. date: 10/23/2015

One

THE BEGINNING

"We'll be on Easy Street, Honey" I said to Bonnie, "if things keep going as they are, the sign at the end of the street will change from Burnwyke Ct. to Easy St." Boy, did I even miss on that one. The time was August, 2011, the slight economic recession that the country had fallen into seemed to be over. My 401K had dropped to about 68 K, but was climbing back and close to 100 K, with no end in sight.

I had worked for the local utility company for 12 years at their nuclear plant on Lake Erie, living in Madison (Ohio), for twelve years while doing so. Prior to that I had worked as a Stress Analysis for a pressure vessel fabricator in Barberton, the major supplier of equipment to the Naval Nuclear fleet. When I left that job for greener pastures, always chasing that pot at the end of the rainbow, I worked for an Architectural/Engineering firm in Independence (OH), as a Pressure Vessel Engineer. I thoroughly enjoyed my job there, but the recession in the early 80's left me high and dry. After scrambling to get work where I could, after all, I had three teenage kids, I ended up with the utility, who moved us to Madison OH.

Well, it had to happen, just when I was getting comfortable at the 'Nuke Plant', management decided to 'downsize', feeling that they didn't need a pressure vessel specialist (I would use 'expert', but I'm not sure I qualified, and I'm too modest). After all, does the nuclear reactor qualify as a pressure vessel, apparently management didn't think so. So I got my walking papers, along with 74 other engineering and technical specialists. Back to square one.

A consultant that the plant used on occasion told me that if I did get laid off, that there was a place for me with his firm in Garfield Heights. This small firm catered to the 'nuke industry'. I contacted him, Tim, and he said that there was a 'power struggle' going on in the firm at this time, and that they weren't ready to bring me, or anybody else.

After looking around for something else I found a firm that needed a Civil Engineer with a Professional Engineering License, so I qualified. The time was Spring of '97, and we were still living in Madison. Bonnie still felt a strong pull to Akron, where her parents lived, along with my family and a lot of our friends, where we were raised. The firm needing a PE operated out of Cleveland, which was about 35 miles west of Madison. Upon starting there, I was immediately sent to the GM Stamping Plant in Mansfield (actually Ontario, OH), but most people called it Mansfield. Now I was 120 miles from Madison, and had to get an apartment, returning home on the weekends.

My supposedly two to three year assignment ended abruptly after six months when GM decided they wouldn't need me after the end of the year. I called my friend, Tim (after all, if he was giving me a job, I had to be friendly with him), and he said that they were ready to hire me. Wow, imagine that, not ever losing work time. So I started working in Garfield Heights, which was only 52 miles from Madison. Unfortunately the distance from home added 2 to 3 hours traveling time to my day.

Not being a spring chicken anymore, nor was my minivan, we started to show wear. Bonnie suggested we start looking around for a home closer to work, and closer to Akron, which made sense to me. After doing extensive research and talking to a number of builders, we found just the right lot in Heritage Woods in Montrose.

Our builder had a model of a home with the Master Suite on the first floor, which we wanted, and needed in anticipation of Bonnie's parents moving in with us. Bonnie had made the builder promise (she had that way about her) that it would be ready by Nov. 1, which he said (in March) that it would be 'No problem'. With the builder living just around the block, she also said told him "My father's 90th birthday is on Nov. 8, and if the house isn't finished, you better inform your wife that we would be having the party at his house". That's how Bonnie was, subtle (as a baseball bat) and firm. True to our builders word, we moved in on Oct. 26, 1998.

Bonnie's parents were great people. Her father, Grandpa Woods, was a very formal type of man, who had an old school work ethic and wasn't afraid to work, even at 90 years of age. Her mother, Grandma Woods, was more feeble, and almost blind, but her mind was as sharp as a tack.

Grandpa still mowed his lawn, and shoveled his walk, and, when we caught him on his roof adjusting his TV antenna, we said, "That's enough!" He rarely raised his voice, and never cussed, smoked, or drank alcohol, from the time that I knew him. He and Grandma attended the Akron Baptist Temple regularly, and enjoyed the fellowship therein.

They lived in a small bungalow in the Kenmore area of Akron, having bought the home in 1934, during the Great Depression, where they raised Bonnie and older sister Elaine. We tried to get them to move in with us, but they were very resistive, stubborn and independent, so there was nothing we could do but to support their independent life style. Since Bonnie's sister lived in Georgia, the burden fell on Bonnie. We were seeing them weekly, so we were able to keep close tabs on their health.

As time went on, we sort of 'settled' in to a regular routine, if you could call it that. To give you a bit more insight to the person of Grandpa, I need to share with you the following. In our front yard we had 2 large trees that the builder failed to remove. Well, Grandpa, being an old tree climber from way back, volunteered to cut the trees down, but exclaimed "I'm not sure I can break up that boulder you have in you yard. I will probably have to take a chisel to it with a sledge to get it down to more manageable pieces."

Bonnie and I looked at each other with shock, probably to hide the laughter that was behind it. I said "Grandpa, we paid $500 for that decorative boulder and had it placed there, we sure don't want it removed. Besides, we don't want you climbing trees!"

He smiled, shook his head, and said "Well, if you say so, I won't". We shelved that idea because we didn't have the money to do it at that time anyway.

Bonnie and I started cruising in 1989, celebrating or 25th anniversary. We loved it! We decided to go on at least one cruise a year, and kept that promise to ourselves. The idea of great meals, exotic ports, great entertainment, warm, sunny beaches said it all. By the time August 2001 rolled around, we were seasoned cruisers.

In March 2000, Bonnie received a special from American Airlines, a 5 day cruise of the Greek Isles, bookended with 2 days in Istanbul and 2 days in Athens, flight included from New York for only $1050 per person. She called me at work all excited, explaining it, trying to sell me when I already had bought it by way of her excitement. I told her to "Book It!" which she did immediately. We then made arrangement to get to New York a day before our flight, just to make sure we didn't miss it.

It was a good thing that we decided to go into the Big Apple a day early, because a bad storm in the upper Midwest caused flight delays into the city, and some people on the cruise had to use the two days in Istanbul to get there on their own, missing the flight out of JFK. In fact some of them never received their luggage at all, because it didn't make the transfer in New York, and by the time it got to Turkey the ship had sailed. We had a marvelous time, seeing things that we thought we would never see, going to Ephesus in Turkey, seeing the home Mary, where St. Paul had promised Jesus he would take her to, and an Ancient Library (Having a senior moment, I can't remember the name). From there we went to Rhodes, and then Santorini, where I bought Bonnie a very expensive gold necklace, with the Greek symbol of infinity going around (the neck).

To say the two days in Athens was breathe taking would be an understatement. We visited the Parthenon, the Acropolis, and several remote temples and museums, each breathe taking in their own right.

August of 2000 found us meeting our daughter, also named Elaine and her family in Las Vegas. Elaine, Michael, Sarah and Megan flew down from Seattle, while we flew in from Akron-Canton. I know, who goes to Vegas in AUGUST!!? Well, we did, and believe it or not, the temperature never got over 90 F. Yea, I know, it's a dry heat. We didn't spend much time in Vegas, in spite of their current effort to make it 'family friendly'. We traveled to Winslow Arizona and caught a train that took us to the southern edge of the Grand Canyon, where we stayed in a guest house overnight, and rode the train back. From there we went to Oatman, along historic Route 66, with a population of 50, that swells to 150 during tourist season. The saloon had swinging doors, there were burros roaming around that would eat carrots purchased at the general store. Truly a good time.

Back to reality, at Christmas time, Bonnie's father fell a couple of times, and was hospitalized for evaluation. Nothing major was discovered, but both of her parents needed help. We had them move in with us, temporarily, until he got stronger and could move around without falling. After 2-1/2 weeks, they returned to their happy house and life went on.

Once again we were able to enjoy a wonderful trip. In January of 2001 we went with friends to Hawaii, which seemed like paradise, with high temperatures in the low 80's, and cooling down to around 70 over night. The beaches, especially on Oahu were great. We also enjoyed the Polynesian Culture Center, which was like an Hawaiian 'Epcot', covering the bigger islands of Polynesia. Later the night, before the show, they had a luau. The show was remarkable in itself, worth the price of admission, with flame throwing batons, (I'm not sure that's what they called them, but that's what they looked like to me).

While working at the nuclear plant I was fortunate enough for the utility to sponsor me as a member of the ASME Boiler and Pressure Vessel Code, on a subcommittee on the design and analysis of pressure vessels. The ASME established the criteria by which every pressure vessel and piping in the USA, and subsequently, adhered to by most of the rest of the world. The Code committees meet four times a year at various cities around the states. Originally they met three times in New York, and one time remotely, places like Atlanta, New Orleans, Louisville, Los Angeles, San Francisco, St. Louis, Miami, and so forth. Members from the west coast started complaining because they had to travel across country three times a year, so the ASME started rotating meetings three times a year, with one being in New York. Normally the September meeting would be in New York, but the year 2001 they decided to have it in Norfolk, VA.

Since there was just Bonnie and me, as our kids had 'flown the coop', I frequently took her with me. We would usually fly in the weekend before the meetings that started on Monday. Management was OK with this, as I paid her airfare, the extra room nights, and for her meals. When we would be in New York, Bonnie would go to 'talk shows', shopping, walks, or just people watching in Times Square. There's nothing else like it in the states, and maybe the world, but I can't speak to the world.

In early September the Committee meetings were in Norfolk, and we stayed on Virginia Beach, which was a short commute to the meetings. We were to fly back on Thursday, with my meetings being over on Wednesday. We were able to do some sightseeing in the area before the meetings began.

On Tuesday, September 11, the world changed. While in a meeting someone burst in and said that someone flew a plane into the World Trade Center. We started speculating about it when someone turned on the TV that was in the room. Needless to say, the meeting was over, but we were mesmerized, like everyone else in the world. We witnessed the second plane crash into the second building. Everybody left, the rest of the meetings were canceled. I returned to Virginia Beach, and we called the airlines to see if we could get an earlier flight back. No luck. All flights were grounded, but we were told our flight on Thursday looked good, but to call before going to the airport. Needless to say, that flight didn't happen. The airlines didn't know when the flying ban would be lifted. We were stuck in Virginia. Bonnie watched the fleet going out to sea that afternoon. Needless to say, security at the base was escalated.

We contacted the motel management and told them that we were not going to check out on Thursday morning, but would be staying another night, needing time to sort our arrangements out. They told us that our room was rented to another party that night, and that we would have to move to a new room for one day, but the motel was sold out for the weekend. We next contacted our rental car carrier, Enterprise, and told them that we were keeping the car, and would be driving back to Ohio, and would drop it off there.

Enterprise told us that our rental was a 'local' car, and that it would cost us over $500 to take the car back, as they would have to send someone to pick it up there. Boy, the good times just keep on rolling. We said we would get back to them. We started contacting other companies, Avis, Hertz, and Budget. They all told us none were available, as local servicemen had been renting them going to bases that they couldn't fly to. We were between a rock and a hard place. Bonnie told one of them, Avis, I believe, "Wait, won't navy personnel be doing the same thing to get here?" When they replied yes, Bonnie said to call us when they had a car that could go to Ohio, one way. Fortunately that happened in late afternoon, so we checked out of the motel on Friday morning.

We drove home, but it was killing for Bonnie's back, which couldn't take long rides, so we made frequent stops. We had rain that started in the afternoon and was still going on at 9:30 when we got home. I then had to 'gas up' and return the car to the airport to get my vehicle, getting home after 11. I didn't realize what impact 9/11 would have on me, my family, personally.

As I had said earlier that the company that I worked for catered to the nuclear industry. Towards the end of the year, nuclear plants usually had excess budgeted funds that they must either spend or lose. Most of that spending was with small companies like the one I worked for, who would do engineering evaluations of systems, or equipment, and upgrade the seismic qualification of them, or recommend what needs to be done to accomplish that. These contracts were small potatoes to the utilities, usually around one or two million, and sometimes even less. They were BIG potatoes to us. After 9/11, all the excess funding that utilities had, got funneled into security upgrades, and not upgrading the seismic qualification of systems or equipment. At the end of January, 2002, I got laid off again. Boy, some people just couldn't hold a job.

After a few phone calls, and I ended up back where I started my career, doing equipment analysis for navy components. I was ecstatic. I didn't have far to drive, and we could stay in our home, in a suburb of Akron.

Ajay, our youngest daughter, in the mean time, drifted in and out of our lives. She had gotten married again and divorced for the second time. She knew that we did not approve of her life style, we were concerned that she was back doing drugs. She would come at holidays, because she knew it was traditional, and she wanted to see her grandparents and other family members who always celebrated with us, as would our son Steven.

Aunt Helen, who had been married to Grandma's brother, was a lovely lady, but her health was deteriorating, and she ended up in a nursing home. Since it was close to us, Bonnie would go there often and sit with her aunt. It was the least we could do, as her son Rick was helping us with Bonnie's parents, as he lived down the street from them. Helen passed away, but Rick was still a part of our support group.

Towards the end of 2002, Ajay called and said she needed picked up at a rehab center in Akron. She said she was there by court order, that she was picked up for drugs, and would be on probation. I brought her home, but that was short lived, for she chose to go back to Cleveland with her druggie friends. Since she was on probation for a year, she wasn't on drugs, but she still ran with a surly crowd. How difficult this was for us as her parents.

Bonnie and I continued cruising for our vacation, going to the Inside Passage in Alaska, and cruising the Hawaiian Islands. We felt fortunate that we could continue to see and visit all these wonderful places, and I could go on for a long time about the advantages of cruising, but this is not a tale about vacations.

Here we go again, right before Thanksgiving, 2003, I got laid-off. Gee, a guy could get a complex. The prime contractor for building the power plants for the Naval Fleet, General Electric, decided that they wanted to do more of the equipment analysis in house, and assume more of the construction liability that the fabricator had, so less engineering needed to be done by the fabricator. Consequently, my job was eliminated. Nice to be out of work going into the holidays. I once again started looking for work, drawing unemployment compensation, but the country was starting to slide into another recession, so nothing was available. Right before

Christmas, Bonnie's father fell again, twice, so we had them come stay with us until he recuperated. Apparently he had an inner ear infection, which affected his stability. Unknowing to us, this was just a preview of things to come.

I continued to look for work, but nothing was available for me, having pigeon-holed myself as a stress analyst/ pressure vessel engineer. The state unemployment bureau, in an effort to get people off the public dole, wanted my to go to college to get an Associates Degree. Just what I needed, me, being a Licensed PE, going back to school to get an Associates Degree. And oh, yea, I had to pay for it myself, and if I got work in the meantime, I would have to stop going to school and take the job. Talk about bureaucracy.

Around May of 2004, Ajay called, and said that she was pregnant, and that she was in the hospital in Cleveland for gestational diabetes. Bonnie and I really didn't know what to think. We thought that she couldn't get pregnant, after all, she was going on 32, and she had been running around since she was 15. I decided to visit her in the hospital, to see for myself. She had a history of making things up, or telling stories, as her brother Steven would like to say, so we didn't really know. She was pregnant, and released from the hospital a couple days later when she got her diabetes stable, and under control.

Boo, Shelly and Dominique

Camp bed time with Boo, Maddie and Shelly

Two

COMING HOME

Our life was about to really change. Around Memorial Day, Grandpa Woods was falling frequently. After a family confab with Bonnie's sister Elaine and her husband Bob, and Grandma and Grandpa, it was determined that it was time for them to move in with us. Grandpa was pretty receptive to the idea, but Grandma said "No!" Of course she didn't realize, or accept, that Grandpa, was doing all the work, cleaning, cooking, shopping, banking, laundry, and taking care of her. The girls told her "Mother, Daddy can't do it any more! You are going to move in with Bonnie and Jim, case closed".

Grandma replied, "I want to stay here until July 11, then we can say we lived here for 70 years!"

"Not going to happen, we will move you into our master suite, and we will move upstairs." We had them pick out favorite furniture and mementos to take, and, two days later we moved them in. Grandpa perked up almost instantly, enjoying some well deserved leisure time. He commented that he liked having meals prepared for him and the 'Misses', as he call his wife. They were wondering why I was around so much, and we finally had to tell them that I was unemployed.

With unemployment benefits about to run out, I was getting desperate, and not being able to find an engineering job, I stumbled onto a van with a sign in the window 'worker needed!' I didn't know what type of work, but I gave it a call anyway. A man named Dan answered, and he told me that he runs an installation crew for American Greetings, where they go into stores and revamp the card displays. After much discussion I told him I appreciated the job, and I started shortly thereafter. Although the job was manual labor, it was very interesting, and I learned a lot, and grew an appreciation for my co-workers.

We were like shadow people, first removing the old display, then installing the new. Most people would ignore us, or not even see us. very few would even speak to us. Maybe they were afraid that they might get pulled into our nether world, and never get out. Of course some people did speak to us. It gave me a rare, albeit brief, glimpse of what the African-American slaves lived with, every day, every hour, every minute of their lives. God Bless Abe Lincoln.

Two months after we moved the grandparents in, Ajay appeared on our door with a two week old baby. Our precious granddaughter Shelly had come home to us, but Ajay had other plans. Ajay said that this was temporary. Grandpa Woods was 'pleased as plum' to have a baby in the house. He loved little ones, ALL little ones, and would just sit and hold Shelly by the hours. We started to settle in, but we still weren't sure if we wanted Ajay here, exposing her grandparents to the crowd she ran around with. Bonnie and I spent much time trying to find an apartment for Ajay and Shelly, to no avail. Bonnie offered them to stay with us, so the die was cast.

Grandpa took to Shelly like a duck takes to water. As time went on, he'd call "Come here, Mugginhead," and toddler Shelly would come running. He always wanted something to do, and, in the summer, we would have him process the strawberries, washing, cutting tops off, cutting them into editable sizes. Shelly would be right there, eating every other one until we would yell at Grandpa that he was ruining her appetite. Everyone would laugh, especially Shelly, who though she was getting away with something. She became the apple of his eye. She would sit with him on the couch in their room and watch the bird feeder outside the window. Her presences helped make his last years happy years.

Shortly after this we got a call from our daughter Elaine, who was still living in Seattle. She wanted to come home and asked if she and husband Michael, along with daughter Megan, and their dogs could move into Grandpa and Grandma's house, since no one was living there. The dogs were the problem, as was the situation of some of the grandparents furniture, which was still in the house. All ended up well with the dogs being kept in the basement and Elaine and Michael selling many of their belongings.

Elaine and Michael moved in, and Michael got a job at 'Thinker Toys', a store in Montrose selling educational toys, really quite a place. Their daughters, Sarah, in high school, enrolled in an upscale art school in Michigan. Megan enrolled in the Revere school district, where we lived. The girls, Sarah and Megan, coined the phrase 'the Greats', in reference to Great Grandpa and Grandma. This was for Shelly's benefits mostly, as she got older, and Bonnie became Nana, and I, Papa.

One day Bonnie was shopping at the local Acme grocery store when she ran across a Charmin promo giving away a small Charmin bear with the purchase of toilet paper. Of course Bonnie purchased it, and gave the bear to Shelly. It was her first in a long list of stuffed animals. We started calling it 'Bear-Bear', which was very creative, I thought. Shelly became very attached to Bear-Bear.

Bear-Bear went everywhere with Shelly, sometimes giving Mom and Nana fits. After shopping at a K-Mart, Bonnie and Ajay returned to the car (with Shelly), and noticed Bear-Bear was missing. Bonnie instructed Ajay to go back and retrace their steps to find Bear-Bear. Ajay returned, without Bear-Bear, saying that she couldn't find it. That was not acceptable to Bonnie, who proceeded back to the store. She told the manager that Bear-Bear was someplace in the store, and they had better find it. Being a slow afternoon (not that that mattered to Bonnie), her employees scurried about and one of them found it under a counter. She returned to the car with Bear-Bear. The next day Bonnie got on line and procured 3 more Bear-Bears as backups.

We had frequented the local Red Lobster, that is as much as our budget would allow. Bonnie and Shelly would split the Ultimate Feast, which included a Lobster tail, Crab legs, and shrimp. Of course French fries and salad came with it. Bonnie would get the salad, while Shelly ate the croûtons. Shelly would get half the legs and half the Lobster, and a couple of shrimp. Bonnie would get the rest. While going there, we became friends with two of their managers, Michael, and (another) Shelly. They immediately fell for (our) Shelly.

While we were cruising, now this is only once or twice a year, Ajay assumed the responsibility for the Greats and for Shelly. This worked sort of' well, as long as Ajay was on probation. When she finished with probation, things got messy, with confrontations usually ending up with Ajay saying "Well, if you don't like what I'm doing, I'll just take Shelly and we will leave." I wanted to call her 'bluff', but Bonnie always relented, keeping the interest of Shelly as her top priority.

Ajay again hooked up with Ervin, the supposed father of Shelly. Apparently he got out of jail, and things continued to get worse. Money started disappearing, and, unbeknown to us, some jewelry started disappearing. Elaine and Michael were struggling, and often missed the $435 rent they had agreed to when they moved in. On two occasions, they brought their rent over and left it on the dining room table in an envelope. When the Greats got the envelope, money would be missing, and usually an argument ensued about who took it, with Ajay insinuating that Steve took it, because he had been in the house briefly.

On a couple occasions, a nice couple living across the street had us watch their house, feed their dog, and gather their mail. Being naive, Bonnie and I would, stupidly, let Ajay do the dog feeding and mail gathering. One time we were on a cruise concurrent with our neighbors being gone, and Ajay would go over with Ervin to take care of the property. In addition to us having missing items and money, our neighbors now had some. In fact, one of their guns came up missing. I confronted Ajay, and told her that the neighbor was going to call the police if the weapon was not returned. I personally made restitution for the $550 that was taken from the neighbors, and Ajay came up with the gun. Unfortunately, and probably rightly so, the lady stop talking to us completely, and her husband will only wave as we go by. Ajay and Ervin were buying drugs, and had pawned all of Bonnie's jewelry that they had taken. By the time we figured it out, the only pawn ticket that we found in Ajay's room had expired, and the jewelry was sold. Gone was Bonnie's expensive gold infinity necklace that I bought for her in Santorini Greece, among other things of significant value. Gone, for pennies on the dollar. To say that we were upset was an understatement. The height of her thievery peaked when she stole $900 from the Greats. We could not tolerate it anymore. I once again made restitution to the Greats, and we issued an ultimatum to Ajay.

Ajay agreed, sort of, and things settled down. But then, Elaine and Michael decided that they were going back to Seattle, telling us at 9:30 one night, that their train was leaving the next day, with Elaine and Megan going back, and Michael staying to packup and move everything back. Shortly thereafter, Great Grandpa Woods fell, and continued to get weaker. We called Bonnie's sister who came up from Georgia. Grandpa died in a nursing home on April 29, 2007. His wife, age 99, was still living with us, but now required closer monitoring. Bonnie's sister consented to come up to stay with her when we would go cruising, being partially aware of the situation with Ajay.

Ajay couldn't stay away from drugs, and after an extended argument, left with Shelly in tow. It was the Fourth of July weekend when we got a call from her. "You had better come and get Shelly, the Police are coming and she should go home!"

"Had she eaten, where are you, what do we need to bring?" Ajay assured us she was alright, and told us where she was. Shelly was filthy, and starving, and 'woofed' down a burger from a fast food joint on the way home, from the west side of Cleveland, where Ajay was holed'up in a two bit motel with some junkie.

The next day Bonnie started calling lawyers to find someone that could get us custody of Shelly. This little girl deserved better than what she had. We got one, and papers were soon filed, giving us temporary custody until the court hearing day. Ajay came home shortly thereafter, and when things escalated, and she threatened us that she was going to take Shelly if she didn't get her way, we showed he two things. The first, the temporary custody papers, and second, the door. Have a nice life. But it wasn't that easy, or that simple. Shelly truly loved her mother, what three year old doesn't, and we needed Ajay to work with us so that she could visit Shelly on a regular basis.

Shortly thereafter we got a first glimpse of how special Shelly really was. Of course all parents feel that way about their children, or at least they should. We had obtained Shelly a passport, and along with our temporary custody papers, went on a Princess cruise out of Ft. Lauderdale Florida. Shirley and Jon, good friends of ours, also went with us. We had heard good things about Princess, and wanted to experience it for ourselves. For those of you that have cruised, you know that probably the only downside, in my opinion is the first and last day.

On the first cruising day, after the boarding card was issued, our picture was taken, with the image being assigned to the card. Next came a 'Welcome Aboard' photo, usually with a cutout of the port and the ship's name. We were then allowed to board, usually with the caveat of 'your room is not ready yet, please wait in one of our lounges'. We usually went up to the Lido Deck (every cruise ship has a Lido deck, don't ask me why, but the do) and would go through the buffet and sit and maybe drink a Pina Collata, or some other type drink with a little umbrella in it. Since we were sailing out of San Juan Puerto Rico, we sat on the deck and listen to a Reggae band playing Calypso music.

It was Monday evening of the cruise, having set sail on Sunday, where every ship has a Welcome Aboard show, with a group of young, energetic singers and dancers, usually doing some kind of Broadway show review. We arrived early at the theater to get a good seat (when we started cruising, these shows would be in a big, smoky lounge, like a cabaret, but the bigger ships opted for a theater sitting, sometimes with two balconies). As the theater started to fill up, a friendly, middle aged couple sat next to us, and the women started to talk with Shelly. As Shelly usually did by just being herself, she charmed the lady, and the next thing we knew, Shelly asked to sit on her lap. The lady loved it, and Shelly remained there for the entire performance. A couple days later, as we were waiting for the elevator, when the doors opened, we were greeted with "Shelly!", by some passengers getting off. Bonnie and I looked at each other, saying, I hope you know those people, because I don't. And so it went, complete strangers to us would speak to Shelly by name. Scary, very scary.

One of our port of calls was Bonaire, one of the Dutch A-B-C islands, which was the smallest, and really didn't have much to offer as a tourist attraction. We decided to go swimming, and Bonnie, hearing that you could feed fish dog biscuits, had brought some along. I was breaking them and giving them to Shelly to feed to the fish. When I ran out, she went to Shirley, who couldn't break them with her hands, so she would bite them in two, and give the pieces to Shell. We cracked up. Shelly yelled "Nana, Shirley's eating dog biscuits!". Even Shirley joined in the laughter.

At age three we enrolled Shelly in preschool, thinking that she needed social interaction with other children. Her teacher, Miss Krista, immediately fell for her. Shelly could communicate, understand, and follow directions, and not give anyone a problem, so what was not to like. Bonnie, in the meantime, felt that the pain in her legs and back was escalating. She sought treatment, and got two cortisone shots, 3 months apart, between her C-3 and C-4 vertebrae. Apparently she had a 'pinched' nerve, and the shots help relieve the pain. She also had pain lower in her back, but that subsided, and we felt that the shots helped that also. Her legs still bothered her, but she said little about the pain, just did less walking.

Christmas came and went, and Shelly started to get sluggish, not full of pep, with what seemed like a lingering cold, or cough. We decided to pull her from preschool, thinking that she contacted something from one of the other children. On January 30, 2008, Shelly complained that her legs hurt, and that she couldn't walk. We took her to the local emergency room, and they gave us antibiotics, saying that she probably had an infection. We took her to her pediatrician, Dr. David Karas the next day, and he didn't like what he saw. He arranged for tests to be run at Akron Children's Hospital. It was late at night, and the hospital wanted to keep her over night, and felt that she probably had Septic Arthritis of the Hip, which they called 'Septic Hip', and wanted to do a tap in each hip joint to verify their assumption. They did that the next day, and determined Shelly had an infection in her left hip (joint), and they wanted to clear it out with another procedure. We OK'd that, and they performed the excavation. They said she was very sick, and that she would need antibiotics administered through a port in her arm 4 times a day, with each application taking a half hour. We were sent home with a medicine pole, and a machine and instructions on how to hook it up. Ajay had cleaned up, and moved back, and had knowledge and expertise on how to do the medicine, having worked in a nursing home at one time in her life. Although Shelly legs got better, she continued to spike high fevers, causing us to take her to the hospital on three different occasions.

Around the first of March, we had the final court hearing on the custody of Shelly. Although Ervin had resisted giving Shelly to us at previous hearings, we had requested DNA testing be done to establish that Ervin was not the father, contrary to his name being on the birth certificate. The results were back, and the judge dismissed him as the father of record and he got sent back to prison. Since Ajay had already agreed to giving us custody, there ware no further barriers, and the judge declared Bonnie and I as 'Legal Guardians' of Michelle Lee 'Shelly' Thornton.

Easter Eggs with Nana

EatingLobsterwithNana

Family with Red Lobster Mgr Shelly

Three

THE DIAGNOSIS

Seventeen days later we took Shelly to see an arthritis doctor, who, asked Shelly to walk across the room. She didn't like what she saw, and said "I want you to go and get an CAT scan, then report to the the Oncology ward, I believe she has Cancer". And so our nightmare began.

The results of the scan came in, and we met with Dr. Patton, the Oncologist assigned to Shelly. Dr. Patton took Bonnie and me into a small, private room, and said, "Shelly either has Leukemia, or Neuroblastoma. Pray for Leukemia." Further tests results would be coming the next day. The results showed Shelly had Stage IV, Neuroblastoma. Neuroblastoma is a malignant tumor of immature nerve cells that usually starts in the autonomic nervous system or adrenal gland and spreads quickly, most often affecting young children. The prognosis at that time was a 5 to 10% survival rate. I would have rather been hit by lightning than been told that.

As the word got out, two guardian angels would be at our side every step of the way. One was our friend Shirley Swires, and the other was Susie Hanes, an old school friend of Bonnie's. She had been a friend of Bonnie's, and once a friend, always a friend. Bonnie had found her and invited her to their class reunion. Now, when we were devastated, Shirley and Susie were there for us. For every doctors visit, every treatment, either one or the other would be there. When they couldn't make it to the hospital, they would call or come over shortly thereafter. They became our crutch. The day after Shelly was diagnosed, they came over and drank with us until we were feeling no pain. Susie's husband Ralph became a frequent visitor. It must be hard for men to show emotions, or go through something like this, because it was always Shirley and Susie that was there for us.

Doctor Patton said that there was a small tumor above her left kidney on her adrenal gland, and that they wanted to remove it before treating her with chemotherapy. So Shelly was operated on, one of many operations that she would be going through on our journey to overcome this dreadful disease. The tumor was removed, and I believed it was benign. Her scan had showed that her cancer was in her bones, through most of her body. They did another procedure, that sounds so simple, but it was a spinal tap, with a rather large needle into the middle of her lower back. Of course, Shelly was sedated at the time. Results of the tap showed that the Neuroblastoma was also in her bone marrow.

Dr. Patton outlined the protocol that is followed for treating Neuroblastoma, the guide lines specified by the American Pediatric Cancer Society. I believe the course of treatment was as follows: (2) treatments of chemotherapy with Irinotecan, followed by extracting her stem cells for future transplanting, then (4) chemotherapy treatments of Temodar. Each treatment required Shelly to be in the hospital at least three days, then every 28 days another treatment would start. Between treatments, we would take Shelly in for counts, where blood would be drawn and the chemistry analyzed and given to the doctors. If her counts were low, she would be given platelets, or white blood cells, or other medications the bring her chemistry, or counts into the normal range.

Well, the first of Shelly's treatment left her ill, so it was six days before we could bring her home. The second treatment was worse, as she spent 10 days in the hospital. It just seemed like our little girl just couldn't fight off the effects of the chemotherapy. Her stems cells were harvested, and were cancer free, which would be necessary for transplanting (stating the obvious). We felt that Akron Children's Hospital was one of the best in the state, if not the country. Unfortunately, we discovered that they did not have the capacity to store cyrogenically, which the stem cells needed, for future use; consequently, they shipped them to Children's Hospital of Cincinnati.

At this time, two more very important people entered our lives. Dr. Laura Gerak, a child psychologist and Reverend Carol Harrison, the hospital Chaplain. The amazing Dr. Laura would go from room to room, playing with the kids that were confined to their room. One day she showed up with a sheet, a jar of white sand, and a jar of sea shells, that she said she collected from Sanibel Island, Florida. She spread the sheet out on the floor, and invited Shelly to join her there. She then proceeded to dump the sand out and then the seashells. She and Shelly played with them, and Dr. Laura promised to bring them back the next time. Shelly really bonded with her.

Reverend Carol was new to the area, and we discovered that she lived relatively close to us. She would play with Shell, and would pray with all of us. She just had that way to relate how we were feeling, and what we were going through. We had invited Rev. Carol to our home for a few meals, and enjoyed fellowship with her. With warmer weather, she would get in Shelly's 'Bouncy House' that we would blow up on our back deck. Carol and Shelly would have a grand old time. She became an integral part of our support team.

Shelly enjoyed watching the animated video "Barnyard". She particularly enjoyed Sam Elliott's rendition of Tom Petty's song "Won't Back Down". She asked if her mother would download it to her I-Pad. She would go around the house with her head phones on singing along at the top of her lungs. It was a real treat, but, unfortunately, she must have gotten her singing ability from me, who couldn't carry a tune in a bag. That didn't stop Shelly. She would sing her heart out, singing with a stern look on her face

"I WON'T BACK DOWN!
NO I WON'T BACK DOWN!
YOU CAN MARCH ME UP TO THE GATES OF PELL,
    NO I WON'T BACK DOWN!"

as a four year old, she didn't quite understand the words, mistaking pell for hell. She performed for Rev. Carol on one of her visits. Carol thoroughly enjoyed it, and would always think of her performing.

After a couple treatments Shelly was returning to her old self, and we enrolled her in the Revere pre-school, which was for children living in the Revere area. June came, and not knowing how much time we had, or, how much time Shelly had, we prepared for a large fourth birthday party for her. We purchased a 36" inch, 15 foot round above the ground swimming pool, set up two large tents, and had about 50 family and friends attend. Shelly had her energy back, and, except when she was in the hospital, would go, go, go non-stop. We older people, read me, would usually be exhausted by nine in the evening, but Shelly continued usually until 11 or so. We usually turned over responsibility to Ajay in those late hours.

Before Shelly got sick we had planned a cruise for April, but the doctors told us to cancel it, because she would be in treatment. We agreed. We asked about our Disney Cruise/vacation in October, and they indicated that should be OK.

After her last treatment towards the end of August, the hospital took another set of scans, in anticipation of doing a stem cell transplant. They called us in for consultation. Not good news. We were taken to a small lounge (boy, I was starting to hate these small lounges) where we were told that her cancer has progressed, and that she was not eligible for a transplant. That we would not have her by Christmas, and we had better go home and prepare. We all were flabbergasted, I mean, look at her, running, playing, except for having very little hair, she was acting like a child, I was going to say normal, but no normal child could keep up with her.

We asked about going somewhere else to get treatment, specifically mentioning Philadelphia, not really knowing the name of the hospital, but had been told by someone that they had taken their child there. Dr. Patton told us that the treatment in Philly was painful, and that she would have to be in isolation for 6 to 10 weeks. We stammered at the thought of her being isolated that long, a four year old, how could we do that, so far from home, with very little support with us. Sure, we knew that Shirley and Susie would make regular visits, but to what avail, as she would be isolated. Our hearts continued to break. What to do?

Bonnie, never one to sit on her laurels, showed how strong willed she really was. She took Ajay to the local funeral parlor and bought a casket, which would be held in reserve for us. She then instructed Akron Children's Hospital to prepare four complete history packages, and send them to: (1), St. Jude Hospital in Memphis, (2) The Cleveland Clinic, (3) Children's Hospital of Philadelphia (CHOP), and (4) Memorial Sloan-Kettering Hospital in New York City. Bonnie had found out via the INTERNET the contact person at CHOP, and had talked to them personally, and was told that the procedure that they used was a stay in the hospital of no more than four to five days. We were beginning to lose faith in Akron Children's. It wasn't a question of an incompetent staff, just the opposite, we felt the staff was very good, but we really didn't have a yardstick to compare. But their lack knowledge of what was available elsewhere was very disappointing.

In the meantime, the Palliative Care team encouraged us to put together a Make A Wish trip, ands gave us information, and said someone would be contacting us. Dealing was an uncertain future regarding treatment, Shelly's life expectancy, caused our heads to spin. And we still had our Disney Vacation/Cruise in October. (we had booked three days at the resort, and four days cruising on the Disney Wonder). The hospital staff encouraged us to move up our Disney package, which really increased our anxiety, as if it wasn't high enough anyway. We decided to go to Disney for our Make A Wish trip, and the accommodations were wonderful. Limo to the airport, first class plane seats for all four of us (Bonnie's sister came up to watch her mother while we were gone). There was a lady meeting us at the Orlando Airport, and escorted us to our rental car. She gave us directions to a fabulous place called Give Kids the World, where we would be staying. It was unbelievably nice, especially for three adults whose world was turned upside down, and a high energy 4 year old girl who didn't know she was dying, nor didn't care. She just wanted to have a good time.

We were given a three bedroom cottage at Give Kids the World, and two days of tickets to Universal Studios, one set for Sea World, and three days for Disney. We were told that if we wanted to go to Busch Gardens in Tampa, tickets would be made available. The amenities at GKTW were unbelievable. Upon arrival, the cupboards were stocked, and there were gifts for Shelly. The facilities included a restaurant, a theater, a miniature golf course, two swimming pools, a giant miniature train display, a merry-go-round, a 'wonder' room, with a talking tree, and anything that any child would like to play with. Additionally, each critically sick child that came, received a star with their name on it, which would be embedded in the ceiling, with a remote machine that could be navigated to the proper coordinates, and a beacon shined on it. They also had the Disney characters and a little train that went around the grounds serving as a taxi. Did I mention an ice cream shop that was opened from 7 AM to 10:30 PM? And all of that was free! Oh yea, every Thursday was Thanksgiving, and after the meal, Santa was at the theater with gifts for all the sick kids and their siblings. Most people don't know about Give Kids the World, and there are no sponsorship signs around, but it is truly a miraculous place. You may visit it, but to stay there you must have a very sick child, and can only stay there once. Their history is worth reviewing.

The temperature in mid-September in Florida was in the nineties, elevating our tolerance level of each other. Even Shelly got in the act, having a breakdown at Disney, wanting to go to Pizza Planet to play games, instead of eating. We decided to stay at Give Kids the World one day and go swimming, with Bonnie's nephew, Steve (Elaine's oldest son) and his wife Sally visiting and enjoying the facilities. All in all, it was too hot for me to bear, and although we had a good time, a great time, I was glad to get back home.

We continued going to Akron Children's, getting counts and necessary blood as needed. They gave her more chemotherapy, at half doses of Iranotecan, which she had received during her first two treatments, which had stopped the cancer from growing, (originally), and hopefully would do the same here. We were told that this is not a solution, that it is a temporary stop gap measure, and that some day the chemo would not be effective.

We heard back from St. Jude, feeling that was the best place for Shelly, that they could help her. But after further inquiring, St. Jude told us that there was no current open protocol that they had that would help Shelly. Bonnie and Ajay felt that St. Jude didn't want to treat Shelly, because she was going to die, and that would hurt their statistics. I was more altruistic, feeling that they had nothing in their magic bag that was different from what Akron Children's had done.

In the mean time, October rolled around, and off we go on our Disney Vacation/Cruise package. To ensure that we didn't miss a thing, we went down a day early. Cousin Rick joined us. Rick, unlike Shirley and Susie, was our backup guy. If we had to be at two places at the same time, Rick was the man we could depend on to drive whoever wherever they needed to go.

After dinner, Ajay and Rick went off to find a bar for a drink, and to smoke. Bonnie was tired, and hurting, and suggested that I take Shelly out for a walk. It was about 7:30, and just starting to get dark when we left. I was tired also, but I figured we would run into Ajay and Rick, and she could do something with Shelly, letting an old man get some rest. As we were walking back, I noticed across the highway a sign advertising 'Mini-Golf', and feed the alligators. Boy, now you're talking. Our mini Golf in Akron does not have alligators to feed. I don't know why, I would think that would be a big draw. Whatever! So off we go. In front of the mini-golf they had a number of lagoons, with elevated bridges above them, and about a 42 inch high fence. We were given a couple of poles to use, no charge, with a string and a close pin on the end. They sold hot dogs, cut up, maybe 2 to a baggie, at $2 per bag. Yeah, talk about a racket. After feeding these gators, and going through about $10 of my money, we started to leave. The attendant said, "Hey, don't you want to see the Alligator show in back, it's free, and will start in 5 minutes." I mean, how can I pass up something that Shelly may like and it's free. So we went back.

They had a much larger 'lagoon, with an island in the middle, and a bridge out to it. The whole thing was fenced off. One of the attendants, Gator Greg, opened the gate and went out on the island. I'm sure you have seen the demonstration where the closing strength of the alligator's jaws being very powerful, while those to open were very weak. After demonstrating, Gator Greg pulled out some black electrical tape, and wrapped it around the jaws of the largest gator they had, about a six foot one, and said, "Who wants to ride a gator?" as he carried the gator out of the pit onto the walk. Once again, my faith in human nature, and in the stupidity of teenagers, did not fail me. Several teens in the audience stepped up, and got on, for their picture, which could be purchased for $20. I saw how this worked. A few newly weds were not going to be outdone by some macho teens, so they, the husbands, stepped up (either the wives were too afraid, or too smart. I voted for too afraid).

After the crowd thinned out, I asked Gator Greg if my little one could do it. Was it safe? He assured me it was. I thought, you know, the 'bucket list' for a four year old isn't too long, so let's go for it. Shelly got on, and held the gator by the snout (?), right where the tape was, and smiled. Snap, her picture was taken. Then the gator decided to flex his muscles, and gesticulated (is that a word?) his tail. Shelly got this look of horror on her face, and, snap, another picture. Gator Greg removed her, and we went over to the monitor to view the results with the rest of the crowd. When Shelly's pictures came up, the whole crowd told me to get the one with 'the look of terror' on her face, so I laid out my $20 for a priceless picture of my little girl. We also received a certificate stating that (blank) wrestled a live alligator. Shelly and I marched back across the highway, where, Ajay and Rick had just returned, and showed them the picture.

"What! Are you crazy!? Are you trying to get our little girl eaten by an alligator? Are you out of your mind?" I thought Bonnie covered that last phrase with 'Are you crazy?' but I didn't want to correct her. Not when she was on a roll. "You're grounded! You can't take Shelly alone anywhere for one month without someone else. One month". I thought, that's not too bad, considering we checked that off her bucket list.

We did the Disney thing, and stayed at one of the resorts on the grounds, and took their ground transportation to see the parks that we hadn't seen 3 weeks earlier, and also revisited the Magic Kingdom. When we went to Epcot, we purchased a small stuffed animal called 'Figment' at the imagination center. A little dinosaur like critter. As we traveled through the Kingdom, we lost it. Since we did not realize that it was missing, when we discovered it gone, Bonnie went the the Concierge and asked if they could arrange for one to be delivered to our suite the next day, as we would not be returning to Epcot, the only place that had them. They said they would see what they could do. The next day, after returning from the Animal Kingdom, we found six different Figments, all sizes, all colors. We figured we would be billed, and that was OK, but when we checked out, there was no mention of the multiple Figments.

We were transported by bus to the ship terminal at Canaveral, and boarding went a lot smoother than it had for Princess. Once again, Shelly's magnetism came through. Every cruise line has a formal night, where the guests get all decked out, and attend a giant party. They also have a number of photographers around with different backdrops. We wanted to get a family picture, not knowing how many more opportunities we would have. While standing in line, waiting, Shelly was literally bouncing around on the furniture, from chair to couch and back to chair. When our turn came, we said 'Come on Shell, let's get our picture taken'.

Shelly responded, "I don't want my picture taken!"

This surprise all of us. Usually she loves a camera. We had been talking to a couple behind us who were on the Disney Cruise celebrating their 25th wedding anniversary, without their kids (Yeah, go figure!). I said, half joking to Shelly "Do you want to get your picture taken with this couple?"

"Yes!" she replied. While I wiped the egg off my face, I looked at the couple with a perplexed look.

"OK" they said, "we can do that." So Shelly got in their picture and smiled. She then got in our picture and sort of smiled.

We later encountered the couple in the hall, and they said they purchased the picture (with Shelly in it). Nothing like having your picture taken with a stranger's child and taking it home to show your kids. Once again, Shelly made friends at the theater, and sat on some strangers lap during the performance. We enjoyed this vacation more, because the weather wasn't as hot. But still, with the Sword of Damocles hanging over our heads, it wasn't the ideal situation.

Great Grandma W in Hospice with Shelly

with Papa, Nana and Mommy on Make-a-Wish

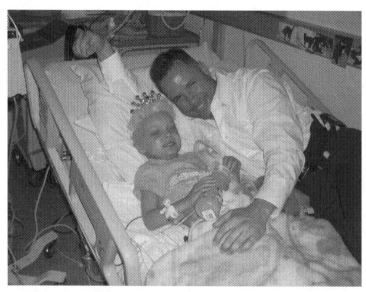

In Hospital with Christopher

Four

OTHER TREATMENTS

When we returned home, we continued taking Shelly to Akron Children's for counts, and platelets, blood transfusions, whatever was needed. Halloween came, and Shelly went Trick or Treating on our street. She was still young, and really didn't get into collecting bounty (yet). We heard from the Cleveland Clinic, and they wanted to see Shelly. We were excited. I mean, aren't they the best in the universe? So we took her there, to see a pediatric oncologist, a very nice and pleasant doctor who looked at Shelly, and then had one of her child life specialist take Shelly to play games while she talked with Bonnie and me. She said what an absolutely wonderful child Shelly was, but there was nothing the Clinic could do, she was "going to die".

Bonnie's maternal instincts kicked in, not grandmother, but maternal, and told the doctor "You're not God! You don't know that. We will get help even if we have to leave the country". So we left, downtrodden and heart broken. Boy, talk about a low. I mean, St. Jude and the Cleveland Clinic both saying the same thing. We were close to losing it.

Thanksgiving was coming, and in the meantime, Rev. Carol had hip surgery, and was told that she could not fraternize with patients while she was recuperating. We were disappointed, but, we focused on our other support people. We were contacted by Jewell Cardwell, a columnist for the Akron Beacon Journal, a daily paper covering the greater Akron area. Jewell asked if we would be interested in taking Shelly on the Polar Express. The Cuyahoga National Park has a train that they operated year round, traversing from North Akron up the Cuyahoga valley to Peninsula, then returning. In the winter, with the help of volunteers, they convert it into the Polar Express, with the volunteers dressing up like elves. Usually the male elf would read the story of the Polar Express, while his female counterpart passed out cookies and hot chocolate. Jewell told us that a retired police sergeant sponsored a car specifically for sick children. We said sure, sign us up.

When we went on the Polar Express, we were greeted by a Grandfatherly elf, Patrick Milo, and his Grandmotherly wife, Helen. Also on the car was Jewell Cardwell, with a photographer. While Elf Patrick gave a booming rendition of the Polar Express story, Shelly looked with wonder out the windows of the many houses that were lit up for Christmas. When we got to the North Pole, Shelly could not take in everything fast enough, afraid that she was going to miss something, with all the elves outside running around, and Santa in a horse drawn sleigh. The Beacon Journal was busy snapping pictures of all the excited boys and girls. As the train returned to the Akron station, Patrick and Helen sat and talked with us about Shelly. They were smittened, as was practically everybody that met Shelly. They asked if they could keep up on Shelly's progress, and we exchanged e-mail addresses. (There was a time when it would have been phone numbers, but I guess I'm showing my age)

Two days later, on a Sunday, there was Shelly's picture on the front page of the Akron Beacon Journal. Little did we know that this was the first of many times Shelly would have her picture in a newspaper, usually the Beacon Journal, but also in local weeklies.

Shortly thereafter, we heard from both Children's Hospital of Philadelphia (CHOP) and Memorial Sloan-Kettering (MSK). Both said that they made no guarantees, but that each felt that they could help with 'Quality of Life'. I struggled with this term, really wondering what it really meant. I found out that, in my terms, it meant possibly prolonged life, and an ability to live them in a normal way, without being bed ridden in a hospital. They both said that they wanted to see her, and do their own assessment prior to treatment. Since the Holidays were coming up, and Shelly's condition seemed rather stable, we decided to wait until after the New Year before we traveled. With all the time I had taken off, and with work slowing up, I decided to retire. Although Shelly referred me as being 'retarded', which I hoped was just a misunderstood word. Everybody got a good laugh (at my expense), but not me.

With relief and hope, before we left for NY and Philly, we went out to eat. We decided on the Red Lobster. Our friends at Red Lobster, managers Shelly and Michael, comped our whole meal, and also gave Shelly a gift card to Toys R Us for $100, and $100 in Red Lobster certificates that we could use in Philadelphia or NYC. They truly loved Shelly.

In February, our granddaughter Megan from Seattle, wanted to visit us, and somehow got permission from school, probably to visit her cousin with terminal cancer, which should be reason enough. She came for two and a half weeks. We contacted CHOP and Sloan-Kettering, and made arrangements to see CHOP on Wednesday, and MSK on Friday, the same week. Shelly, recalling all the fun she had with Dr. Laura and seashells, said she wanted to go to the beach and collect sea shells. So, prior to doing our hospital visits, we took off for Florida with our two granddaughters, Megan and Shelly. Ajay stayed home with great Grandma.

We flew into Tampa, and were met by Steven Tyrone, Elaine's oldest son, and stayed with him and his wife Sally for a couple of days. They let us borrow their pickup truck for our journey to Sanibel Island. In actuality, we stayed close to Sanibel, at Ft. Myers Beach. Our idyllic concept of sun bathing on a warm beach in Florida in February was crushed. The temperature never got up to 70 F, and with a constant breeze blowing off the Gulf, it was down right cold. Shelly, being a typical kid that loves swimming, stayed in the motel pool, but, even that was cold. The only consolation was that it was 'protected' (it had a fence around it.)

We drove to Sanibel Island, and found the beach with shells on it (actually all the beaches had shells), and, braving the elements with sweat shirts, went to gather shells, with our little plastic pails and shovels. Apparently Shelly couldn't tell sea shells apart from sea gulls, as she continually tried to herd the gulls on the beach, in spite of signs warning 'Do Not Disturb the Gulls' or some such thing. We could always claim ignorance in that Shelly couldn't read if the Shore Patrol came by, or the police. Shelly would run towards the flock and they would light out and land maybe 50 yards away, only to have Shelly run towards them. As Shelly got farther up the beach, we had to go and lasso her back towards us. In the meantime, those of us who were not corralling Shelly, were gathering shells. Two bucket fulls, which were going back on the flight with us. We returned home, and had a couple of down days prior to our trip to the hospitals.

Bonnie and I then took our granddaughters on a road trip, first to Philadelphia, then to the Big Apple. Never having been to Philly before, we didn't know what to expect. CHOP was/is one of the premier children's hospitals in the country, which we were soon to learn. I'm going to give you the laymen interpretation of their treatment, so, even if you hold my feet to the fire, this is how I understood it. They told us they use a chemical that they labeled MIBG. It's stands for a 24 letter word, that once you hear it, you'll use MIBG also. My understanding is that the 'I' in MIBG is Iodine, specifically I-131, which is a radioactive isotope of Iodine. I was told that most hospitals use MIBG as a diagnostic tool, because I-131 attaches itself to the cancer cells. It is usually administered one day, and the next day or two, depending on the hospital, they take a radiation scan of the subject, and the Iodine will show where the cancer is located. This was the procedure used by Akron Children's in determining the growth of Shelly's cancer. I later learned that Iodine 122 is actually used for diagnostic purposes, but I digressed. CHOP uses I-131 for treatment. The philosophy being that if the Iodine is attached to the cancer cell, and radiation can kill these cells, then let's use the I-131 to kill the cells. The problem is, 'How much?' without killing the patient. They had been working for over 20 years to refine the procedure so that a universal protocol could be used. They told us that Shelly would be in a paper lined room to stop the radiation particles, which were Alpha particles (I'm showing some of my Nuke expertise), which are the weakest radiation particles giving off in a nuclear reaction. Her bed would be shielded with four lead boards, looking like chalk boards on rollers, but substantially heavier. The life monitors would be rolled to the door, where the nurses could monitor without going into the room. Since the MIBG had a half-life of 25 hours (there I go again with the nuke stuff), it was shipped in from it's manufacture (in Canada) the same day of the treatment.

It usually arrives around noon, and the procedure would start shortly thereafter. The MIBG would be administered through her Broviac port. After the procedure, a Tech would take a radiation reading with a Geiger Counter, and Shelly would not be released until she was not a danger to the public, which was usually around three or four days. We asked if we could be in with her, and they said yes, but we had to dress with paper jump suits, and wear booties and gloves, and record what dose we received on a dosimeter. We thanked them, and told them we would be in touch, still needing to go the Memorial Sloan-Kettering.

As we left and talked among ourselves, we felt that this was a long way from the six weeks of isolation that Akron Children's told us would happen.

The next day we saw the Liberty Bell, and got an original Philly Steak sandwich at Pat's, the winner of the 'eat off' with another restaurant close by, both of which were claiming to have the best. We then traveled to New York via the Jersey turnpike, where, as we got closer to the Big Apple the more unreal the traffic became, moving a mile and a half in an hour and a half. Once through, we high-tailed up to the upper east side, where the Ronald McDonald House was located, on E76th street. By the time we got there it was 7:30, so I dropped the girls off and asked about parking. The person behind the desk stifled a laugh, and said they did not have parking but I could park on the street. Yea, right. We had our big, full size conversion van, which wasn't ideally suited for the big city, or any city for that matter. Finding a place on the street was a lost cause, so I turned into the first parking garage that said it had openings. The attendant came running out, waving his hands, saying "Your van is too big! I can't accommodate you". So off I go, around the corner, down the street, getting farther and farther away, until I found another garage. Like Yogi Berra said, "deja vu, all over again". I was getting desperate. I came back to near the Ronald McDonald House, where there was a garage on the corner. I pulled in, the attendant came out and said "I don't have any room"

I told him "I'm staying at the Ronald McDonald House down the street, where else could I park?" That must have been the key, he knew that we had a sick child. He asked how long would I be staying, and I told him two nights. He said, alright, but he would park me in the back. I was instructed to remove all valuables from my van, and give him the keys. Wow, what a deal, and for only $53 per night. The room at Ronald McDonald's was only $35 a night. (more digression, the Ronald McDonald House we stayed at in Philly was the first Ronald McDonald House built, and the one in New York was the largest, a 13 story high rise.)

The next day found us in the children's clinic of MSK. We met with their chief oncologist, who talked about MSK's approach to curing cancer. Apparently mice have antibodies that will kill cancer cells, at least Neuroblastoma cells, and they try to reduce a patients resistance to a foreign object, in this case the mice antibodies, and then insert the antibodies into the patient. They also were trying to 'make' human antibodies to kill the cancer. This work, like that at CHOP, was developmental, so only those patients who were desperate'would they take. We told the doctor that we were not given any direction by any professional, that we still didn't know what course of action to take. He smiled, nodded his head, and said that he understood. He recommended that we go to CHOP for treatment, then, when we were done there, and that they couldn't do anything else, to come to MSK. Wow! We finally had some guidance. We thanked the doctor, and before we left, took the girls to see the Statue of Liberty, and Ground Zero. We then returned home, ending our road trip.

Megan returned to Seattle, and we focused on getting Shelly to CHOP for treatment. But along the way, Grandma Woods took a turn for the worse. She was having trouble breathing, and was placed in the hospital with Pneumonia. She recovered, but continued to get weaker. After much discussion, and input from her doctor, who said that she's on a downward spiral, we had her placed in Hospice. So now we have two terminal patients to care for. We made arrangements with CHOP for Shelly's treatment, while we continued to shuttle back and forth to Hospice to see Grandma.

Bonnie decided that she would stay home and be with Grandma, while Ajay and I went to Philly with Shelly for her treatments.

Once again, we drove, apprehensive about the weather, but it was clear and just cold that first week of March. We stayed at the Ronald McDonald House, and proceeded to CHOP for the treatments to start. They started on March 4, a Wednesday, and were as advertised. Dressing out, lead shielding, dosimeters, the whole works. Shelly was released on Saturday, but, they needed to take a scan to see where all her cancer was. And, the scan people didn't work on the weekends. So, back to the Ronald McDonald House, with Shelly in tow. Hold your horses. Shelly couldn't be around other vulnerable children and still be emitting radiation, albeit within national guidelines, so they made arrangements for us to stay at a nearby Sheraton. Even though the Sheraton had a better suite, and we didn't have to make the bed, we would had rather stayed at Ronald McDonald's for the fellowship with other people, and for not having to worry about meals, but it was what it was.

On Sunday, being a day off, we went to the Philadelphia Zoo, which was nearby, and the weather cooperated, being in the upper 40's. Monday found us back at CHOP for a scan, then on to home. Word from Nana said that Grandma was stable.

We continued to get Counts at Akron Children's Hospital, and needed platelets or other blood products. In April we were contacted by (elves) Helen and Pat Milo, who told us about their son, Christopher, who was a concert pianist, and that he was performing at the local Barnes and Noble, and said they would like to see Shelly, and to have Christopher meet her. We said "No problem, we will be there".

When we arrived, Christopher was already playing on the balcony, where about 40 or so chairs were set up, and around 25 people were sitting and enjoying his music. Shelly loved going to Barnes and Noble, specifically to ride the escalators. To her it was an amusement ride. She would go up and cross over and come down. How can you tell her not to continue, it was on her bucket list. Strangely, she could never differentiate between the words escalator and elevator' She combined them and came up with 'elligator'. She knew they were different, but felt they had the same name.

When we entered, Shelly made a beeline for the up 'elligator' with us trying to keep up. Our good friends, Susie and Ralph had joined us, and we all reached the top just in time to see Shelly walk across the balcony and sit next to Christopher while he was playing.

When he finished, he turned and said "Hi, I'm Christopher, what's your name?"

"I'm Shelly!"

"I've heard about you. I'm sorry you're sick" replied Christopher

"I'm not sick, I just have Cancer, I call it my bug"

"Well I'm sorry you have a bug" marveling at this spry little girl with little or no hair.

"That's OK, because I get a lots of hugs because of my bug" (Boy, from the mouth of babes.)

That moment in time inspired Christopher to start a non-profit support group for cancer victims and their families, call Hugs N Bugs. Soon after he came to the house and talked with us. We told him Shelly's history, about not having success with the chemotherapy, and how we were turned down by the Cleveland Clinic and St. Jude's. He was shocked, to say the least. We later learned that he had a contract with St. Jude's, to write and make a music video for them about cancer and the families going through treatment.

Christopher told us that he cancelled his contract with St. Jude, because they had refused Shelly. He said that he still was going to make a music video, and wanted Shelly in it. (It can be found on the Hugs-N-Bugs site – www.hugsnbugs.org – under multimedia, called "Side by Side Meltdown"). So, with Grandma still in Hospice, and Shelly still getting counts once or twice a week, Christopher wanted us to take Shelly to the local Portage Lakes State park for filming. Bear in mind, this was the end of April, so there isn't a lot of water activities happening in northern Ohio.

Bonnie and I always enjoyed eating fish, as there is nothing like a good fish fry, with all you can eat fish. (I guess my West Virginia heritage is showing). One Friday we had invited Susie and Ralph to join us. We picked them up and went and stuffed ourselves to the gills (pun intended). On the way back, Ralph was sitting up front we me, Susie was behind Ralph next to Shelly in her car seat, and

Bonnie was in the far back of the van. There were two conversations going on. Ralph and asked me what Shelly's middle name was. I told him it was Lee. He said that was his middle name also, and turned to Shelly and said "Hey Shelly! You and I have the same middle name".

Shelly replied "What's that? Mugginhead?" with sincerity. We cracked up. You never knew what Shelly was going to come up with, but from that time on, Ralph was called 'Mugginhead'. When ever we needed comic relief, Shelly was sure to brighten our days. God how I loved that little girl.

Towards the end of April, Akron Children's took scans of Shelly, working closely with Dr. Yael Mosse of CHOP. They told us the results looked good, but we would have to get the official word from Dr. Mosse. She called us shortly thereafter, and told us that most of the Cancer was gone, and recommended that we return to Philly for another round of MIBG. We made arrangements, and on May 10, the day after Mother's Day, and Bonnie's birthday, Ajay and I once again departed for Philadelphia, not really worrying about the weather this time. Bonnie wanted to stay home with her mother, who was moved out of the Hospice Insurance umbrella, to regular insurance (Medicare). Hospice knew what we were going through with Shelly, so they were flexible with Grandma's treatment and care, knowing she would be returning to Hospice sooner or later. While there, Bonnie talked with one of the volunteers, MaryBeth, who told her about a special camp for kids with cancer called Camp Quality Ohio. We had been disappointed that the camp associated with Akron Children's stipulated the starting age of 6 years, and with Shelly being just 4, she would not qualify. Marybeth told Bonnie that Camp Quality took kids at 4 years old.

Our trip and time in CHOP was uneventful, and because of a policy change, staff was on hand for Saturday scans, so we came home on Saturday. Once again, Shelly was being monitored by Akron Children's on a weekly basis, and more often if her counts were low.

Although Camp Quality runs a weekly camp for kids with cancer and their siblings, they also do other things year around. One of them is a bowling day at a local facility, with pizza being supplied, and craft volunteers being there. Bonnie and I took Shelly, with Ajay being with Grandma at Hospice. At the bowling activity, Jewell Cardwell was there, with a photographer. Yeah, go figure. Guess who's picture was in the Akron Beacon Journal again. I would come to say that Shelly never met someone that she didn't love, or a camera that she didn't like.

Because Shelly had been having excellent 'counts' readings, we requested that her (external) port, a Broviac, be removed, and an under the skin Mediport be installed. With summer coming we knew that Shelly would want to be swimming, and she couldn't do that with a Broviac.

In early June, Bonnie's sister, Elaine, came up from Georgia to see and be with her mother. It was felt that, with Grandma being 101 years old, that she wouldn't be around much longer. She was just getting wore out. We found out details about an African Animal Reserve, near Sandusky, and went with Aunt Elaine and good friend Shirley in tow.

We arrived, and went in and paid. They also sold us a bag of six carrots (for $4.00) that the grazing animals would eat from our hand, through the window of our vehicle as we drove through. Shelly wanted Shirley in the front seat, and sat on her lap. We started to break up the carrots to make them last longer, as we felt that they were expensive. We drove through, laughing and amazed at the hoofed animals. There were Water Buffalo, Gazelles, Llamas, Alpacas, American Bison, Zebras, and others. Since our admission was for the whole day, we decided to get some Lake Erie Perch sandwiches. After enjoying our sandwiches, we bought a 2 lb. Bag of carrots at Walmart for $2.00. We went back to feed more animals. Once again, Shelly was on Shirley's lap. We stopped and a big Alpaca (or Llama, I can't tell them apart) stuck his head in their side window, with Shelly just cackling as she feed him a carrot. Well, our not so friendly Alpaca chose to regurgitate the carrots, all over the inside front of the van, getting on Shelly, Shirley and yours truly. Shelly laughed so hard so peed her pants (on Shirley), as we shooed the animal out of the window. Shelly, along with the rest of us (maybe not Shirley) was roaring. Shelly then said "I'm going to be sick" from the carrot bits all over her, so we grabbed the plastic bag that the carrots came in for her, and, as she emptied her stomach, we realized the bag had a hole in the bottom, and that went all over Shirley.

We were dying. Shirley said "Boy, am I glad I came along for this fun day!", as she also laughed. As we left the compound, we got out and went to their petting zoo, well, everybody but Shirley, who went to the restroom to clean up.

Three days later we went to Medina County's Relay for Life walk, where Christopher had arranged for Shelly to be the Grand Marshall. Christopher was playing at the meal so he had some pull with the officials. Once there, Shelly, and every other survivor of Cancer was given a Tee-shirt to wear for the parade. Apparently Shelly thought it was going to be a race, as she took off like a bullet, and when she was 50 yards down the loop, everyone else was only half way there. She stopped, turned around, and yelled "Come on!", to the pleasure of all the survivors. Bonnie sister participated in the walk, as she is a survivor of breast cancer. Later in the festivities, they awarded Shelly a purple Guitar, as she had told Christopher that she wanted to be a Rock and Roll Star when she grew up. Shelly had a blast, going booth to booth getting things, with nobody accepting any payment for them.

Grandma continued to get weak. To compound our hectic life, I wreaked our van. Well, I didn't wreak it, some old man turned left in front of me while I was running a YELLOW light. Even though the police cited the other driver, Bonnie never forgave me for wreaking her van. This was the vehicle that she ran around town in, grocery shopping, local doctor visits, going to the hospital and to Hospice. The insurance company provided us with a loaner, until they would cut us a check, as our van was totaled.

Life was moving fast. The latest scan from Akron Children's Hospital showed NO Cancer. None. Zero. Zilch! We were ecstatic. Bonnie was getting Shelly ready for Camp Quality, something we all were excited and anxious about. But Grandma took a turn for the worst. She died on July 7, 2009, at 101 years of age. Truly a full and wonderful life. She was where she wanted to be, in Heaven with Jesus and Grandpa. We took Shelly to the showing of Grandma on

Saturday, then on Sunday delivered Shelly to camp. To say that this camp is amazing is an understatement. Each Cancer child and their siblings gets assigned a Companion, a volunteer, usually a college student, but often somebody taking a week's vacation from their job to be there with these kids. Shelly's companion was a pretty young lady, Karla. Karla was a second grade teacher, and had come to the house to break the ice with Shelly. They bonded instantly. Now understand, Shelly had not yet turned 5 years old, so we didn't know how she would do for a week away from her mother, Nana and Papa. Maybe more significant, was how would we do without Shelly around? We tried to stay busy, and brought in my brother's son, Terry, to paint Shelly's room pink. We then decorated it with a fairytale castle transfer on the wall, and took out her youth bed and put up a four-post bed. We added a large 'SHELLY' on the wall, a room truly for a princess.

When Shelly returned home, she was speechless. She totally loved her room. But she still slept between Nana and me most nights. She talked about how wonderful camp was. She didn't get home sick until Wednesday, when she called around 10:30 at night and just wanted to talk to us. She didn't want to come home, just wanted to hear our voices. We were proud of our little girl. The Camp Director, Kerri Frank, told us that while other girls in her cabin usually crashed around 9 PM, Shelly and Karla would come over to the Director's cabin and watch TV with them or play cards, usually retiring around midnight, but sometimes falling asleep there. They didn't admonish her, or even get upset. If that's what she wanted to do, that was fine with them. Wow! What a great attitude.

We had planned a big birthday party for Shell, on July 26 (two days before her birthday), but on the prior Monday, we got a call from CHOP saying that they had a new protocol that they wanted Shelly in, and that she had to be at CHOP at 9AM on Wednesday. To further complicate things, she needed to go the Akron Children's Hospital and get EKG of her heart, and we were to bring a copy with us (on disc). Well, hello! How do you call and tell a hospital that you need a procedure done immediately. I mean, they have other things to do. Come on. Well, CHOP said they would call and grease the way for us, so at five o'clock we were getting an EKG at Akron Children's, and waited for a copy. We hurried home and packed, with Nana going this time. Ajay wanted some down time, so she decided to stay home.

We made it, even stayed at the Ronald McDonald House. Then on Wednesday we were at CHOP at nine o'clock, I'd say sharp, but even Shelly looked a little tired. One of their great child life specialist came out and took Shelly to a play area, while Nana and I went with Dr. Mosse to her (small) office. Also there was her PA, a nurse, a social worker, and the hospital chaplain. They closed the door. Bonnie and I were beginning to get nervous. The last time we experienced this scenario was when Akron Children's told us Shelly had Cancer. We looked at each other, wondering what was going on. Dr. Mosse walked over to us, and standing in front of me said "We reviewed Shelly's file, and feel Shelly is NOT eligible for this new protocol"

"What?" I demanded, probably the first time that I took the lead. "What do you mean?"

"In order for Shelly to be eligible, she has to have traceable cancer. We can't find any" said the good doctor. "I believe we can CURE her".

Bonnie and I both broke down. There was hope for our little girl. Thank you Lord. "OK, what needs to be done?"

"We feel that Shelly should have a stem cell transplant".

"OK. Can that be done here? Can we get started tomorrow?" I said anxiously.

"No, no." came the reply. "We can do it here, but we must prepare. We must get insurance approval, among other things, so go home and we will be in touch".

So we went home, ecstatic, and still not knowing what lies ahead. CHOP applied to Ohio Medicare, who was paying all of Shelly's bills (maybe it was Medicaid, I always get the two mixed up), to get authorization to do the transplant. It was rejected. We even appealed, wanting to get it done there, but they said No, after all, it could be done in Ohio, as Akron Children's had already received permission a year earlier. We weren't exactly enamored with Akron Children's, as they had told us Shelly was not going to be around for Christmas, and for sure didn't help us find CHOP. We decided to look around Ohio, still babes in the woods about even the names of children's hospitals, let alone the size, quality of staff, capability of doing stem cell transplants, and Lord knows what else. We searched the web, and came up with Cincinnati Children's Hospital, Nationwide Children's Hospital in Columbus, and Rainbow Babies and Children's Hospital in Cleveland. Because Shelly's birthday party was that weekend, we put the phone numbers on the back burner until after the party.

Another typical party for Shelly, with about 50 people invading our house, kids running and swimming, plenty of food, just a general good time, as Shelly was feeling good. The next Monday, Ajay started calling the Hospitals, getting to the Oncology ward and having a person of authority call us back. Dr. Kenneth Cooke of Rainbow Babies called us back on Tuesday, saying they had a whole transplant wing. He was the head of Transplant and many other areas. He said he wanted to see us the next morning, at 9 O'clock. He had cleared his docket, (slate), whatever you want to call it, and devoted the whole morning to Shelly and us. Talk about closing a deal, we were sold, signed on the bottom line, everything. He told us that they wanted to do their own scans, and that he would have his assistant schedule them. We left, fat dumb and happy. Well, at least I was fat, and dumb. We were all happy.

On our first clinic visit to the University Hospitals Rainbow and Babies Hospital, we were ushered into a small exam room, where Lucilla Mack, a nurse who was assigned to Shelly, greeted us. Lucilla was a nice, pleasant woman, who startled Shelly, and rightly so, as Shelly threatened to kick her if she gave her a shot. Lucilla said "I'm going to take you out behind the shed and we will see who's the boss. There will be no kicking!" Shelly meekly accepted the shot, and the bond between the two was made. Shelly would want only Lucilla to administer shots from there on out. Dr. Kenneth Cooke entered, a tall good looking man, who commanded every room that he walked into. He hit it off instantly with Shelly, and was amused at the vitality of our little girl, who was climbing off the bed onto the window sill.

Messin' with AJ

Five

TRANSPLANT AND RECOVERY

While we were waiting for things to fall in place at Rainbow Babies', we didn't sit around idle, twiddling our thumbs. Shortly after our visit to Rainbow, the Circus came to town. Or at least Richfield, which is close enough to call our town. We got tickets, and went in the morning to watch them raise the Big Top, using the elephants for the heavy work. We had a couple of hours down time before show time, so we went to the local Cracker Barrel for breakfast. Going back to the grounds about an hour before show time, we walked around and looked at the animals and bought stuff. Bonnie, still not able to get around well went and got in line, where she met a nice middle aged couple and proceeded to tell them Shelly's story. We showed up and they talked to Shelly and us and were smittened by Shelly, like most people that meet her. We went in and decided to get seats at the top, because there was a backrest. Well, that couple from in line ended up next to us, and, you guessed it, Shelly sat on the gentleman's lap for the whole show. At the end of the show the Ringmaster announced that there would be elephant rides at the elephant circle. Shelly shouted, "I wanna ride! I wanna ride!" So off we went, well, actually Shelly went off with the man, into the mass of humanity, while we looked at each other wondering what just happened. Did a stranger actually go off with our little girl? Was he actually taking her to the elephant ride or slipping her to his car? We spread out, Ajay going to the elephant ride, Bonnie hanging back, and I took off for the parking lot, just in case. Actually, the only person moving fast was Shelly, as the rest of us were trapped in the mass exodus, including the man and his wife. We all finally met up at the elephant ride, including the man, and Bonnie, Ajay and myself breathed a sigh of relief. Shelly rode an elephant, with the stranger that sat by us. Go figure, all she ever rode with me was a camel (one hump, is that a dromedary or an Arabian?) at the Cleveland Zoo.

The next week, while we were returning from a restaurant, my cell phone rang, and I answered. It was the Akron Children's Hospital telling us to come in for scans and other tests in preparation for the Stem Cell transplant. I asked if they were doing it for Rainbow Babies, and they said no, they were planning to do the transplant. I said "Whoa! We never authorized it to be done at Akron. We are having Rainbow Babies do the transplant!"

They responded, Dr. Patton, Shelly's oncologist, that since we were going to have the transplant done at Rainbow, that we can have all the follow up and counts done there also. We didn't know that hospitals could be so parochial. Akron didn't have a problem with CHOP, and they worked with Cincinnati Children's, where they had Shelly's stem cells stored.

Two days later we received a letter stating the same, signed by Dr. Patton and the chief Oncologist, Dr. Hoard. So be it. It seemed logical anyway, to have everything being done at the same hospital.

The staff at Rainbow scheduled surgery for Shelly to have a Broviac port reinstalled. A grandfatherly head of Surgery, Dr. Barksdale, performed the surgery. He inserted it below her left breast, stating that some day this young lady will want to have a strapless dress to wear to the prom, and he didn't want any scars showing. What a great philosophy for a doctor. No wonder he was head of surgery. About a week later, prior to the scans, we went to Geneva on the Lake, where Bonnie and I used to visit when we lived in Madison while I worked at the nuke plant. Ajay spent a lot of her time there while in high school. I once heard it called 'The poor man's Myrtle Beach'. Our old friend, Kris Meek of Madison came over and visited us. We swam in the motel pool, played putt-putt golf, and went to Funland, which had a Merry-Go-Round and motorized paddle boats (is that redundant, or just an oxymoron?). Shelly just couldn't get enough. She wanted to go go go. Bonnie watched, and sat most of the time, still being bothered walking and doing things.

With one weekend left before transplant, we went to Cedar Point, where our neighbors Bob and Jan had their boat parked. Bob went with us into the park. Shelly was bummed out, she just wasn't big enough to ride the big coasters (thank God, because I probably would have been forced to ride them with her, with Ajay getting sick on coasters). She cried, but was sort of pacified as we watched the fireworks from their boat deck. The next day before we checked out of the local motel we were staying at, Shelly had to go swimming in their pool. Being in the 60's didn't deter her. (It deterred me, with Ajay having to step up).

With September, Shelly was admitted to Rainbow for her scans, and for the start of her transplant. Although it was explained to us, we still didn't understand the severity of the procedure. Shelly had three days of extreme Chemotherapy, with each treatment taking about two hours. The chemo was suppose to kill the remainder of cancer hidden in her body. It also killed everything else. Her immunity cells, and everything else. She lost her hair, her fingernails, her toenails, she developed ulcers throughout her system. All of this came after the fourth day, the day they transplanted one bag of her stem cells that had been harvested at Akron Children's and had been (cyrogenically) stored at Cincinnati Children's.

Shelly shortly thereafter started a temperature of 104 F, which lasted for over two weeks. She was one sick puppy. With cooling IV solutions, and ice bags, she was drugged most of the time and slept. The doctors at Rainbow allowed us to listen and participate in daily rounds, unlike Akron Children's. They continued to report that Shelly was progressing, and that the high temperature was as • predicted, and had been told to us. Her visitors were limited, and those that came, came for support for us. Although Christopher Milo did come for Shelly, and was able to get her to smile, the first we had seen since before the transplant. She loved Christopher.

Shelly was in Rainbow for six weeks. In addition to Christopher visiting, we had regular visits by Susie and Mugginhead, and Shirley. On one occasion, when we knew for certain that Shirley was coming we told Shelly. This being the first time Shirley drove herself to the hospital from Akron. For those of you that don't know Cleveland, Rainbow Babies is located on the east side, at University Circle, and is part of the Case Western Reserve Medical Center Hospitals, just down the street from the Cleveland Clinic. The Ronald McDonald House that we stayed at was between them, sort of, and offered shuttles to both complexes. The Cleveland airport, Hopkins, was on the far southwest side of Cleveland. We received a call from Shirley that she was leaving, and Bonnie told her to park at the Ronald McDonald House, that she would meet her there and ride the shuttle with her back to the hospital. After waiting about a half an hour, Bonnie took the shuttle back, in anticipation of Shirley arriving shortly, based on a typical 45 minute drive from Akron. We waited an additional 45 minutes, figuring that Bonnie and Shirley would be walking in the door anytime, when the phone rang, and it was Shirley.

"Hey! I'm here by the airport, how much farther?"

"Shirley, you went the wrong way! Didn't you follow my instructions?" I said as I shook my head back and forth.

"No, Jon did a Mapquest for me for the shortest route. I must have made the wrong turn," Shirley said "I knew I shouldn't have relied on him!"

I gave her instructions, and an hour later she walked in with Bonnie, cursing in 'Shirleytalk' "Geez Ow Frog" was one of her favorite expressions. Never a cuss word. That's OK, her presence brought a smile to Shelly's face.

Shelly came home in mid-October, and was feeling pretty good. We had to be careful though, as she had no immunity, we had to keep her from crowds, so having her go to Kindergarten was out of the question. She could go the following year. We celebrated Halloween, with Shelly still going only up and down our street. She wasn't a big candy eater anyway, she just liked to get gifts.

Our traditional Thanksgiving dinner had changed, as Grandma was no longer with us. We had Cousin Rick and Steve join us for the usual turkey (and ham), and all the fixings.

December 6th found us on the Polar Express again, but this time Elves Helen and Pat were on a different car. However, Jewell Cardwell and her photographer were there. Once again Shelly made the Beacon Journal (I truly believed Jewell loved Shelly, and being so photogenic, so did her photographer).

Christmas time was fun. Lots of toys and gifts from all visitors, and parties to go to, although we had to watch where there was going to be a lot of kids present. Little did we know that this was our last 'Joyous' Christmas. My brother and his wife, Terry and Geri brought my mother to help celebrate. It was a happy time.

In February we felt Shelly could get a little exposure to the world, so we went to the Red Lobster to see our friends, and to eat, of course. We talked with Shelly, the manager, while one of the waiters took Shelly out to see the lobsters. They would get the lobster out of the tank, and give Shelly a crayon and have her put it in the claw, and then turn the lobster loose on the floor to walk around with a crayon. Shelly was tickled. And the fact that the stem cell transplant seemed to work tickled the rest of us.

Shortly after that we went to Christopher Milo's studio, where another cancer victim, 13 year old Emily, was. She had wanted to record a song the she composed for her Make A Wish. Bonnie told her mother, Angela, to do something fun. She would arrange with Christopher for him to record her song. They had done that, and they enjoyed their visit to Orlando. While at the studio, which was a photo op, Shelly got restless, and wanted to do something. In the small studio, with probably 4 other adults, those part of Christopher's entourage, with a couch, a couple chairs, and a coffee table, Shelly wanted to play duck-duck-goose. We and Emily's mother watched, the rest of them ran around the table, the couches, through the studio, wherever, playing the game. It was hilarious. We all ended up rolling on the floor, not really, there wasn't enough room, but you get the idea.

Shelly wanted to go to Florida again, so in March we flew to Orlando. We stayed at the Econolodge a couple days, and returned to Universal Studios, where Shelly and I rode the Jaws boat ride twice, and ate a great shrimp meal at Bubba Gump's. From there we drove to Tampa to visit Cousin Steve and his wife Sally, whom we truly loved, and stayed with them for a couple days. While with them, we went to a local county fair and Shelly rode her first Ferris Wheel. She loved it, just a preview of things to come. I may have trouble convincing her that the eligator was a ride.

We returned, and about the Ides of March Shelly entered Revere's preschool, for a couple of months.

We finally got to have a Mother's Day and Birthday celebration for Bonnie, who felt that she was always cheated out of them. Since they almost always coincided with each other, we had always celebrated our mother's Mother's Day, and it seemed like Bonnie's birthday was an afterthought. Several times I tried to make it up to her by taking her on a cruise at that time. We would celebrate with our mothers before. Since my brother was taking my mother out for Mother's Day, we stayed home and had our celebration. I guess it was Ajay's turn to get overlooked. Shortly thereafter, Camp Quality had their bowling bash, and we attended, at least Shelly, Nana and I. Yeah, you guessed it, Shelly appeared in the Beacon Journal again, this time in her pink 'tu-tu', all proud and everything for throwing a strike.

In June we surprised Shelly with a Nickelodeon Cruise. She knew we were going on a cruise, but not that it was a Nickelodeon one. This one sailed out of the Port of New York and went to Bermuda, then the Bahamas, then Florida then back to NYC. We went to New York a day early to see if we could see Buddy, at Carlos Bakery in Hoboken NJ. Buddy was the star on his TV show The Cake Boss, which we all had watched. Once again, granddaughter Megan had flown in from Seattle to join us, with Ajay opting for a vacation with her boyfriend. Good friends Jon and Shirley joined us, although Jon followed a day later because of a previous commitment. We met Buddy's sister, who let us take pictures of her and Shelly, and then marched Shelly and Nana to the back room to meet Buddy personally. They showered Shelly with gifts. A tee-shirt, an autographed picture of Buddy, and two videos of the show. Shelly was tickled, as was the rest of us as we enjoyed their very tasty baked goods. Jon met up with us that evening, and the next day it was off to the port.

We boarded and sailed to the Bahamas on a very large Caribbean Cruise Liner ship, 'The Explorer of the Sea'. This ship was huge, displacing 140,000 tons, over a thousand feet long, 3800 passengers, I mean, like Wow! It had a central walkway, with fountains, and plants. All these little shops to take your money. An ice ring, with open skating, and a ice shop. It had a rock climbing wall, and a mini-golf course. Plus a huge theater. Following the standard format of all the cruise lines, they had a Gala Welcoming show in the theater the first night. Surprisingly, Shelly did not sit on the neighbor's lap during the show. It wasn't until the second show that that happened. We had brought Shelly's skates, and Megan skated with her during open skating.

In the Bahamas Bonnie needing some rest and pain medicine decided to take a leisurely walk into Nassau and seek out the Farmer's Market. Megan, Shelly and I went to the Dolphin encounter at Atlantis on Paradise Island, the BILLION dollar resort built by Merv Griffin, and currently owned by some oil rich Sheik. We also went swimming, with Bonnie taking a less arduous path to go shopping with Shirley and Jon. It's not that often that you can ice skate and swim on a tropical beach in the same day. Another item crossed off Shelly's bucket list. Shelly had also been incorporated into the ice show, 'The Enchanted Castle', and was pushed around the ice on a sleigh. We also made a port stop at Cape Canaveral, and took an air boat ride.

Upon returning to port, we gathered all our luggage and took off, with Shirley and Jon following us. When we were about an hour out of port, I received a call on my cell phone stating I picked up the wrong bag, that they had mine (actually Megan's) right there, with my phone number on it. We confirmed it and returned to port, with Shirley and Jon going on home. Fortunately for us, Megan's mother, Elaine had put my cell phone number on her bag label, knowing that their home phone number in Seattle would not be of much help. After switching the bags, and apologizing profusely, we left (again) and arrived home around 10 PM. I still had my girls, and they were in reasonably good health, so all was well.

We started getting Shelly ready for Camp Quality, and her new companion, Kelly Doyle, came to our house to meet us and Shelly. Kelly was a beautiful, young nursing student at Capital University in Columbus, and she was eager to meet Shelly. She was also worried about trying to replace Karla, Shelly's last year companion, who just had a new baby. She felt that she wouldn't measure up to Karla. We told her, "Kelly, you'll do fine. Shelly loves everybody. Just be her friend, and give her love, and you'll have it made." Kelly reluctantly agreed, but soon learned that it was true. The two had a blast at camp. No late night phone calls. No worries. Shelly was a veteran camper, everything went well.

We had Shelly's sixth birthday party, with all the trimmings. Kids swimming for two hours, the food, party, games, pinata, and clean up (woo, glad to get it over).

At the end of August, Shelly started Kindergarten in the afternoon. After the second day riding the school bus, she secretly told her mother that she kissed a boy on the bus. Her mother, never able to keep a secret, told Nana and me. We had a good laugh, but with all kinds of 'sexual harassment' going on, we told Shelly that she shouldn't do that again. That evening, while taking her to the park, she told me, "I didn't kiss him one time Papa, I kissed him twice!" I swerved, unable to keep the car on the road.

I asked her who this boy was, and she said "Nicholas. I told him he was my boyfriend!"

More swerving. I thought I was going to have the big one. I didn't think that I would be having this talk on her second day of Kindergarten. Maybe when she was 13, or hopefully 16, but SIX! Come on! But the irony of it all, was that he would be her boyfriend through thick or thin. The dye was cast.

The last Saturday of August, Camp Quality had arranged tickets for all the cancer families to attend 'Buckin' Ohio', a rodeo in the thriving metropolis of Burbank, population 1312, and one traffic light. An outlet mall opened up, so they added another traffic light, but the mall was called "Lodi Station" after another town close by. I guess Burbank Station just didn't have the right ring to it.

We went, and there was a big tent for the Camp Quality people, which was fortunate, as it rained, and rained, then it poured. They had horseback riding for the kids, and Shelly wasn't about to let a little water dampen her spirits, so she rode and rode until the attendant gave up and said "No more! Please." The rain stopped, and we watched the rodeo, but then Shelly got tired, and we left.

But not before she tried to talk us into going to the Outlet Mall. We prevailed, and Shelly fell asleep before the mall was out of sight.

Camp Quality activities continued, as in the middle of September they had a fair with a bouncy house and slide, music, a clown making balloon animals, face painting and food. The Beacon Journal had a photographer, and Shelly's picture made it again. I lost count the number of times her picture has appeared, I know more than mine has, which was once, when I graduated from college as the 15000th graduate. Boy, what a distinction.

Yearly Camp Quality Ohio, along with Camp Quality Michigan, meet at the Kalahari Water Park, just outside of Sandusky Ohio. Twenty five cancer families are invited from the Ohio camp, of which we were one of them. Ajay 'opted' out at the last minute, so we invited Kelly to join us for the two night, two day fun. In addition to the room being provided, we received admission to the water park, and Camp Quality supplied meals for everyone. Bonnie spent time in the hot tub, which helped with easing her pain.

Bonnie was still in a lot of pain, so we found a doctor who specializes in pain management, and I took her to see him. She received ultrasound treatment, acupuncture treatment, massage treatment, and still didn't receive much relief. With Shelly as our top priority, Bonnie decided to live with her pain.

Our manager friend, Shelly, from the Red Lobster got transferred to the store in Wooster, which just happened to be near an ice ring. With our Shelly wanting to go ice skating now that she has the 'bug', we went to Wooster, first to skate, then to visit the Red Lobster. Shelly, the manager, was very pleased that we went out of our way to find her, and she 'comped' our meals (that wasn't the intent, Shell wanted to see her).

At Halloween, I took Shelly to 'Boo at the Zoo', since we had a yearly pass, and we visited frequently anyway. The zoo had a number of volunteers dressed up at various locations passing out candy. Some noticed that Shelly had very little hair, so she received extra candy. Not that she ate any, but she enjoyed receiving gifts. Almost always in our visit to the hospital, be it Akron Children's, or Rainbow babies, or CHOP, Shelly, and the rest of the kids in the oncology department, and probably all the children would receive gifts at each visit. Shelly loved stuffed animals, and her collection was starting to rival 'Toys R Us'.

Once again we had Thanksgiving without either of the 'Grands'. I was thankful for my girls, and felt that Shelly was going to beat her cancer. On the Monday after, we went to a large charity function, Project Ed Bear, which was established by Susan Summerville, and her husband Skip. The Summerville's had owned a business furniture store in south Akron, and Great Grandpa Woods (Bonnie's Dad) had worked for them. Susan contacted Bonnie, and said she would like something that Shelly 'created' for the auction. The function was held at Quaker Square, a very large dining hall, with everything top shelf. The hors d'oeuvres were wonderful, and there was a large number of valuable items available for bidding. Shelly's item, a ceramic Santa sold for $125, which we thought was good.

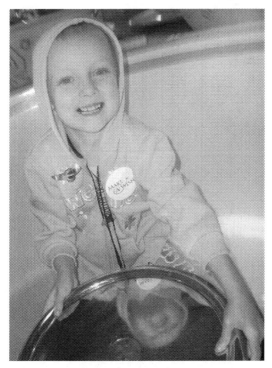

On Make-A-Wish trip

Proper attire

Punk rocker

Shelly with Great Grandma T

Shelly wrestling live gator

Shelly with Rev. Carol -4th Birthday

Six

RELAPSE

In December it was Polar Express time again. This time Ajay joined us. One of the guest, volunteer conductors was a former neighbor of ours, Polly Bowman. Polly continued to show up for Shelly's parties and at Halloween, always bearing gifts. This wonderful lady truly loved Shelly (yea, I know, here I go again), but Shelly had that way about her that makes people want to love her (I don't know how to explain it, she must have been born with it, because she didn't get it from me). As Shelly watched with wondrous eyes (once again) out the window at the lights, and the Christmas displays, I felt a 'calm' come over me. My little girl was going to beat her cancer (and I call her 'my little girl', because she wasn't just my grand daughter, she was even more than a daughter to me, just based on the bond that we had, maybe because I spent most of my awaken time with her). Little did I know, the other shoe was soon to drop.

One of Shelly's Camp Quality friends, Olivia Ward, had succumbed to her cancer. We knew that the time was imminent, but it was still a shock. Children, our precious children were dying from cancer, and there wasn't a damned thing we could do to stop it! I took a step back, still feeling blessed that my little girl was beating it. I wrote a family Christmas letter stating that we thanked God for Shelly being in remission, after all the treatment that she had been through. I normally don't do the Christmas letter thing, feeling that some of the ones we receive are over the top. Two days after mailing them, Shelly came home from school, sick. We felt it was just the flu, but we took her to the local ER anyway. The doctors felt the same way, and told us to keep her out of school the next day.

The next day she was sleeping and moaning on the couch. We called Dr. Cooke, and he told us it sounded like the flu, but call him that evening with an update. At supper time we tried to wake her up for some soup. Didn't happen. She wouldn't wake up. We called Dr. Cooke and he said to take her to the local ER (again) and have them call him directly. Five minutes late I was barging through the ER door, carrying Shelly. This couldn't be happening! They called Dr. Cooke, and reported that she was non-responsive. He said for them to prepare her for transit, as he would send Lifeflight down from Cleveland to take her to the University Hospitals complex, of which Rainbow was a part. As they were working on her, I called Bonnie, and told her to pack things for them and that I would come and get her. Ajay, in the meantime, was vacationing with her boyfriend at Myrtle Beach. A call to her and they said they would be leaving the next day for home.

I picked Bonnie up and returned to the ER just before Lifeflight arrived. As they prepared Shelly for transit, I told Bonnie to ride with her in the helicopter, that I would drive to Rainbow and catch up with them there (we almost always referred to the UH complex as Rainbow, even though it's a conglomeration of about six different hospitals). I took off, and not traveling over 80 MPH, (honest) I beat them to the hospital. They arrived shortly and rushed Shelly into the PICU (called 'pick you', for Pediatric ICU). A young female doctor came out and told us a scan showed a tumor on her brain, at the base of her brain stem. She said they were going to drill a hole in the top of her head to relieve the pressure which was causing her unconsciousness, and to get her stable for surgery to remove the tumor. While waiting, the life specialist that controls Buddy came by. She was ready to leave for home, but chose to stay with us. She said that she wanted to be with us until things got stable. Around 11, we encouraged her to go home, and shortly thereafter, Dr. Cooke showed up with his able assistant, Linda Cabral. They gave us an update, saying that we had a very sick little girl, but everything was being done that could be done. I believe they left for home shortly thereafter, but I'm not sure, being in such a fog, wondering how we got here, and what was going to happen.

I tried to rest on a four foot couch in the lounge, and around 2:30 AM the young female doctor came out and said "I think we are losing her! We can't get her blood pressure back up" Apparently they had been giving her medicine to reduce her blood pressure, and when they drilled into her skull, blood 'squirted' out, and her BP dropped radically, and they couldn't get it to go back up. Bonnie said "We're going to see her!" To which the doctor replied, "Let us get her stable before you do, there's one more thing we are going to do."

"You don't understand, I said we are going to SEE her" and Bonnie pushed pass the doctor and went into the ICU. By the time we got to the room, her blood pressure had risen to 80 over 40. I was told later that it had bottomed at 40 over 20. Shelly wasn't out of the woods yet, not by a long shot. Shelly's heart had been stressed by the tumor and the subsequent low blood pressure, and then the medication to bring it back up. Shelly's little body had been traumatized, and not operating at full capacity.

The chief ICU doctor, a nice doctor name Dr. Toltzis, kept me up to speed on the progress, or the lack of progress of Shelly. He said that Shelly must be stable, and be able to stay stable in the face down position, for the surgeon to remove the tumor from the back of her head. Ajay arrived the next day, along with a lot of support people, family and friends like Shirley and Susie. Dr. Cooke checked regularly on Shelly. In fact he questioned one of the medications prescribed, and Dr. Toltzis told him "Ken, you're going to have to take a step back, let us do our job". That's how much Dr. Cooke loved Shelly.

On the second day, Olivia's parents, Bill and Lillian Ward contacted us and said they wanted to come and bring us some food that very day. Bonnie told them "Not today, you just buried your precious daughter today, you can't do this too. Please, come tomorrow or the next day" Which they did.

Six days later the doctors felt Shelly was stabled enough for the surgery to take place. Her blood pressure was close to normal, and her heart was as good as they felt it needed to be. Her surgeon was Dr. Coen, and he was assisted by another Dr. Coen, his wife. They successfully removed the tumor, and had it biopsied. Results showed that there was just a tiny bit of Neuroblastoma present. The surgeon, Dr. Coen would later go on to be Chief of Surgery at Mass General in Boston. He was/is one of the best.

One night while I was staying in PICU, with Bonnie and Ajay over at the Ronald McDonald House, Dr. Toltzis came to me and said "Do you have any more of those 'lucky stars' on hand?" because Shelly had surely needed one to pull through. I sort of smiled, if you can smile with a little one, or anyone for that matter, in an ICU recuperating from brain surgery.

Shelly spent another week in PICU, before she was stable enough to be moved to a floor at Rainbow. Although visitors were limited in any ICU, Shelly seemed to have a steady stream of people. Kerri Franks and Carol Cross came from Camp Quality on Christmas day. I can't say enough about the camp, or the staff. If everyone had the philosophy of these people, everybody would be singing Louie Armstrong's song "What a Wonderful World It Would Be". Although Shelly had only spent the fall in school, her Principal Katie Kawza and Vice Principal Beth Harrington both visited. As did her Kindergarten teacher, Mrs. McLean, who not only brought us food, but, unfortunately had an accident on the way home from the hospital. Others came, it appeared, by the bus load. Of course our friends, but family also. And, of course, Christopher Milo came. With his shenanigans, he got the first smile out of Shelly, post surgery. I could feel the love, but we still needed Divine intervention.

Shelly was moved to a new wing in Rainbow, and we settled in, waiting for a complete recovery. In addition to the visitors that came, there was a steady flow of medical personnel. The surgeon and his staff came; as well as the Anesthesiologist and his staff. We had asked for a dentist to look at her teeth, which were giving her trouble. Because of the location of the incision, Shelly's 'gag reflex' was malfunctioning. Consequently, the therapists that specialize in swallowing came. The physical therapist, Kevin, came. He had worked with Shelly during her transplant, so we knew he was helping her. Nurses would come and take blood. Technicians would come and take her for more scans. It just seemed endless. Shelly couldn't take it anymore. Who could blame her? She started being resistive, insisting that people leave her alone. One night, late, the door opened. I was staying that night. I think I stayed most nights, because I needed to be there with her. Shelly was asleep. I jumped up to intercept the person coming in the door to say 'No, no more tonight!' when Dr. Barksdale stuck his head in the door. I was surprised, but also glad to see him. He was a special surgeon, who care about his patients. I'm not implying that there are surgeons that don't care, that is wrong, but he was special. As I told him Shelly was sleeping, he commented "I won't bother her, just tell her the IDIOT was here", and left. I cracked up. Shelly was an equal opportunity insulter, never discriminating.

The next evening, a nurse came in around supper time, and said she needed to draw blood, but not from her port, but from her arm. I didn't know the difference, but I guessed there was one. My little girl was going to be hurt again. Shelly was fighting, crying, but I relented and let the nurse take her blood. She said they wanted results for rounds in the morning. Since it takes 24 or 48 hours to grow a culture, I couldn't understand the logic. Then, at midnight, the nurse appeared again. Waking Shelly and me up, I demanded to know what was going on. Same story. Hold your horses right there. You are not going to take anymore blood from Shelly in the middle of the night. It's not going to happen. The nurse finally left, without blood. At 6 AM the next morning, guess what? A different nurse, the shift hand off had taken place, and another intended poke. That's it. I wanted to throw her out, literally, and I almost did. I know, she was blindsided by me, but Lord have mercy, give my little girl a break. She left, mumbling something about the doctors not having results for rounds. That's OK, I thought, I will talk to the doctors on rounds! The doctors explain, after I calmed down, that Shelly had an infection, and that they needed the cultures to determine if the antibiotics were working, or if the dose should be increased. I asked why three cultures, and they said one was enough (not really answering my question).

As Shelly worked to get her strength back, she was getting nourishment through her IV, and a feeding tube through her nose. She was still one sick and hurting little girl. Eventually, Dr. Barksdale surgically implanted a feeding tube, as getting proper nourishment was a problem. Around this time, Shelly was getting very restless, and going to the game room daily wasn't satisfying her restlessness. We received special permission to have her boyfriend Nick visit. He came, and laid in bed with Shelly and talked with her. It was very endearing. Shelly was also missing her cat, Smokey, whom she hadn't seen since before Christmas, and it was now late January. Dr. Cooke really bent some rules, and allowed Smokey to visit. One could tell that they both missed each other. Smokey crawled up in bed with Shell and just licked and licked her, his way of showing affection.

Near the end of January Shelly's strength was at an acceptable level, but they wanted to give her spot radiation treatments, where the Neuroblastoma could still be present. In order to treat the exact same spot, a plastic mesh face mask was made of Shelly's face. Her face mask would be bolted down for the treatment. They wanted to give Shelly 10 or 12 spot radiation treatments using the mask. But a strange thing happened on the way to the treatment room. The doctors felt that Shelly didn't need to be in Rainbow Babies for the duration of the radiation treatment, but she did need further therapy for her gag reflex. Consequently, Shelly was transferred to the Cleveland Clinic's Children and Rehab Hospital, which was nearby. So off we go. Shelly with Ajay, Nana and myself in tow. Oh yeah, and the semi-trailer of gifts and stuffed animals. In addition to the ever present 'Bear-Bear', there were 4 other stuffed animals that she liked, and played with. The leader was a plaid, hippie type monkey, called 'Monk', then there was (we weren't sure) a critter with a Mohawk haircut, that Shelly called C.J., for Christopher Junior. She also had an elephant named 'Elle', a cat name 'Whiskers' and finally, a sleeping dog that she used as a pillow, aptly named 'Pillow'.

When she went by a shuttle back to the UH complex for her radiation treatments, the techs were wonderful, from Nick and Diane to Terry and Candy. The child life specialist, Jeff, would frequently show up. Although Shelly knew that a reward was awaiting her daily, she still got bored during the half hour procedure. I was told that I could talk to her through a intercom, although she could not be heard by us. Well, I warmed up my vocal cords, and did a slap stick routine of truck drivers on their CB radios, which just happened to be the same frequency as a local air traffic control tower, talking planes into and out of the airport. For the most part, Shelly smiled. It helped her get through the procedure. The staff enjoyed the monologue, (I think), they said something about be being on a stage (the one leaving in ten minutes).

The first time Shelly had radiation treatment the year before, upon daily completion, she would race Candy or Terry down the hall to the gift box. This time around, we pushed her in a wheelchair. You could see the pain in the people's eyes. The doctors wanted Shelly to get more Chemotherapy, so that would begin after we got released from the therapy hospital.

We still had not celebrated Christmas at home, and with progress going slow with the gag reflex therapy, we wondered when we would be going home. We begged, pleaded, and I was not above bribing, but it never came to that, to get a one day pass so that we could celebrate Christmas at home. Remembering that when we came to the hospital, we had most of our gifts purchased, but not wrapped. Not that Shelly needed anymore gifts, but we weren't going to tell her that. Ajay went home a day early to wrap gifts, and, so, on Super Bowl Sunday, Feb. 6th, we got a one day pass, with the promise that we would be back by 6 PM. It had something to do with the insurance, that if we could take her home longer, why does she need to stay in the hospital? We had family and friends come over, and I believed I prepared a ham for sandwiches for everybody, but I'm not sure. By six o'clock we were back at the rehab hospital, ready for six more days of therapy, and the Super Bowl. Needless to say Shelly received more gifts and stuff animals. (I thought about adding an addition to the house)

Shelly started with more Chemo, with treatment in the hospital, and then being released three days later. She also received an additional twelve rounds of whole body radiation, not like that received at CHOP, but it did require us to shuttle to the hospital daily for the 12 days, with each treatment being about 20-30 minutes long. Shelly enjoyed getting things, not that she played that much with them once they were brought home. As was the case, with all the other visits to the hospitals, she would ask about a prize, or where's the prize closet, and would go and pick out what she wanted, sometimes more than one. Our house was being overcome with toys, especially stuffed animals.

We were going down the recovery road but it was a little bumpy. Shelly had only one radiation treatment left, as she started another round of Chemo, which would be her last Chemo medicine until after the CRUISE! Yep, we're going on another cruise over spring break (March 27 through April 3). Shelly was losing her hair, but wasn't too upset about it. It could be because she looked forward to her mother having her head shaved (for St. Baldrick's day, where people shave their heads to support cancer kids). Ajay was going to do it in Kent the following weekend. Shelly was struggling with a cough and cold, as well as keeping some food down, and possibly a urinary track infection. Chemo has a way of messing up your immunity. The early morning treatments (having to be at Rainbow Babies at 7:45) had taken it's toll on everybody, but it's was almost over. Shelly pushed the envelope, wanting to go, go, go, both before school and after, but, it was wearing her out (to say nothing of us old timers). She still got one feed bag a day, which helped, as her appetite was sporadic, at best. She went to school, but missed a couple of days, either just tired or under the weather with her cold. We encouraged her to try to go, because we couldn't gage what level of discomfort she was going through, and we thought being with the other kids would help get her mind off of the bug. God helped her through this time, because she loved to go to school. And they were glad she was back. Her Mom and Nana went to school on Thursday to see a book parade. It was really cute, all the kid had books for the parade.

Bonnie's pain had not subsided, but that didn't keep her from doing what she loved, for those she loved. She found a cruise that featured the Nickelodeon characters on the Norwegian Jewel, but it was not a Nickelodeon Cruise, the difference being that the stars of 'iCarly' and other teenager shows weren't on this one. SpongeBob and Patrick,

along with Dora the Explorer and other characters were.

We drove to Ft. Lee, NJ on Saturday and had a great visit with Kim and Chuck Blakely, fellow cruisers that wanted to see Shelly again. We had met them on our Bermuda cruise, and Shelly had sat with them during one of the shows. Bonnie had decided to look them up, only knowing that they lived in New Jersey, near NYC. She researched the phone books and called a number of Charles Blakely's in northern New Jersey until she found them. Kim was shocked that

Bonnie had found her. (I wasn't). They showed up with a Barbie and (Shelly's first) Ken doll, which Shelly played with off and on during the cruise. We had a great visit with them, and they were pleased to see how well Shelly was doing. We tried to get to Carlos' Bakery (even though we knew Buddy, the star, was in Akron, of all places on Saturday - yea, go figure). But it turned out that Carlos Bakery was giving away cupcakes, and the line was 3 blocks long, so we passed on the cupcakes, although we dropped off pictures for them taken previously with Shelly.

We went to the ship and arrived around noon, which was a good time for boarding. Thanks to our cruise planner, Dick Davidson, who's really a great guy, he arranged for welcome aboard wine and chocolate covered fruit. Shelly still didn't know that it was a Nickelodeon cruise, as the characters weren't present to welcome us. At one of the early shows it was finally revealed to her. She just looked at Patrick with a strange look. Nana asked her 'do you know why Patrick is there?' and she said that she didn't. Nana then said 'This is the Nickelodeon cruise that you wanted to go on' and she almost fainted. Although our reservations for breakfast with the characters was lost, we got to go thanks to a head waiter named Roman. Another customer facilitator, Rochelle Brown went out of her way to make sure Shelly had maximum fun and got to meet SpongeBob, Patrick, Dora, Diego, and Avatar. The staff from Nickelodeon was great. We also cannot thank one of the photographers enough, Gabriela (she's too nice to be called by her name tag 'Gabby'), for helping us with all the pictures and asking her boss to give us all our pictures (or, as she put it, our memories).

Shelly still did not eat well on the cruise, she did thoroughly enjoy the air boat ride and Alligator refuge that we went to in Canaveral, although she tired in the afternoon. On their private beach she enjoyed building sand castles and swimming, although the water was cold, the 80+ temperature made it acceptable. At Nassau, we went on a glass bottom boat ride. Nana was having trouble with pain in her back and legs, so we got a wheelchair from the ship, and I pushed her to the boat ride. The walkway was very bumpy, and it jarred Bonnie as I struggled to keep up. Shelly was so tired again that she sleep through most of the Glass Bottom boat ride, only to become a power shopper in training at the Straw market, where, if she didn't buy anything, the women would give it to her. The women were so taken by her that they showered her with gifts. I kid you not, she ended up with 6 hats and 13 necklaces, among other things. More importantly, they also promised to pray for our girl.

She was in awe of the performance of a couple act named 'CrazyHorse', who competed on American's Got Talent, and performed acrobatics from ropes and drapes. She also loved the magician, Jean Pierre, who gave her a DVD and an autographed picture, after performing a personal show just for Shelly (he also gave her his magic deck of cards, although they look normal to me). We hated to leave, but we gave many kisses and hugs to members of the crew and the Nickelodeon staff that fell in love with our princess. We will never forget this wonderful cruise. When we left to go home, there was no luggage mistake this time, we learned our lesson, or at least I did.

On leaving NYC, I got a call from my nephew that my 92 year old mother had fallen and had fractured her eye socket, her cheekbone, and her pallet, and was in Akron General Hospital. Ajay refused to show me the picture that he sent, fearing I would lose control of the car. Feedback from my brother was sketchy, but apparently she had fallen, and possibly laid in the hall of her small house for up to 14 hours, before being discovered by a neighbor. Boy, the good times just keep on rolling.

Additionally, Shelly lost one of her teeth Sunday on board, and another one Monday on the school bus (boy, the gig of the tooth fairy was getting expensive). Shelly went to the doctors on Tuesday, her counts were good, but she has lost weight. She also lost a cap on one of her teeth, so we had to go to the dentist Thursday. Everything was OK for time being, but she was back on Chemo (for 5 days every 28 day period).

My mother was released from the hospital after a week, and taken to the Copley Health Center for therapy, as she had hurt her left arm and leg during the fall. Since that facility was only around the corner from our home, it was convenient for us to visit.

Shelly, of course, was remembered from the time the 'Greats' had been there, although not at the same time. She liked visiting their rabbit, Herbert Hoover, and feeding him carrots. She also joined the Tuesday evening Uno card game. She became quite good, which I would expect, seeing as how I taught her (not bragging, just fact).

Shelly had not been Shelly since she got sick in December, so we decided to stop the Chemo treatments. As far as we knew, there was no traceable cancer, but we would get updated the week of May 9th, when Shelly underwent a complete set of scans, tests and whatever else the doctors decided to do. The Chemos were making Shelly very sick, both with vomiting and diarrhea, and she wouldn't eat (which was understandable), even if we fed her through her tube, she would throw it up, as she lost 4 pounds (10% of her body weight). Just the last few days we had seen a small spark of our Shelly, with her eating well enough to gain back 2 lbs. Earlier in her diagnosis, when Shelly had a hard time gaining weight, we rewarded her with a trip to Chucky Cheese when she got to 40 lbs. We once again offered her that prize. We prayed that she remained cancer free, as that particular type of Chemo really hit her hard. She needed time to regroup. Hopefully, the cancer would remain in remission, but if it came back, we prayed that there would be another type of Chemo to fight it.

Shelly fatigued easily, and her liver enzymes were high. The doctors said that there is a sleep syndrome (I forget it's name) that is common to kids that have radiation and chemo treatments. Twice she fell asleep on the school bus coming home. Although this gave us more time to relax (if one can relax with a child that has cancer), it also gave us cause for concern, as this is not the Shelly that kept us going. Additionally, she was not eating, and we had to give her a feed bag nightly to keep her weight up. She was hovering at 37-1/2 lbs, and we wanted to see her back at forty (for another Chucky Cheese party).

The high liver enzyme required an additional blood test, and fortunately, we were able to get it drawn locally at a UH facility close by, not requiring an additional trip to Cleveland. Results show that her reading has dropped, and her liver should recover by itself over time (according to the doctors).

Sleeping with Smokey

with companion Kelly

Seven

BONNIE'S CANCER

In the spring of 2011 Shelly's school, Hillcrest Elementary, approached us, saying they were wanting to raise money for 'The American Cancer Society', and 'Hugs N Bugs'. Christopher Milo had performed there at Shelly's request, and the school was very impressed by his message and wanted to support his cause. The principal, Katie and/or vice Principal Beth, asked if Shelly could help pass out ice cream cupcakes to raise money for fighting cancer. Of course, Shelly wanted to. Being in the afternoon kindergarten, they requested Shelly be there early to accommodate the morning kindergarten. We took Shelly, and after doing the double shift, Shelly asked if we could stay around so that she could get early release (from school).

Bonnie spoke up, saying "No Shelly, I'm sorry, but I'm in so much pain that I need Papa to take me to the ER, so you will have to ride the bus home". Our ER visit revealed more than we wanted. The X-rays and and a CT scan revealed a mass on the back of her right lung, which had two nodules rubbing the rib wall, causing the pain. After seeing her family doctor, and a few blood tests, she went to UH hospital in Cleveland and got a bronchoscopy and a PET scan. The results of the scan and test showed she had Small Cell Lung Cancer and it had spread to her hip. We had more blood testing to do, and we went to see an Oncologist (Dr. Lois Teston), to plan on how we were going to attack the cancer. Dr Teston said that Small Cell Lung Cancer was very aggressive, and that without treatment, Bonnie had only 6 months to live, that with treatment, she had a year. Bonnie was reluctant to get the recommended Chemo, but that was part of the regiment, along with radiation, so we encouraged her to fight the good fight as Shelly has fought it.

Shelly still remained sluggish, and was sleeping a lot, and not eating much even at her favorite Red Lobster, where we celebrated

Nana's birthday. We hoped she would come out of this malady soon, as it wasn't like her to sleep 15 hours a day.

In the mean time, Shelly had to have a series of scans, again at Rainbow Babies and Children's Hospital. Shelly passed her latest scans with flying colors, i.e., everything came back negative. We were so grateful and was optimistic that Shelly's sluggishness would abate soon.

I was becoming very cynical at this time. It was hard to stay upbeat for a 6 year old terminal cancer victim, even with the cancer in remission, and a wonderful wife of 47 years who was told by her oncologist she will probably not see her 48th anniversary. (our anniversary was the following Monday). She said the cancer has metastasized into Bonnie's other lung, her spine, and her kidney. Although this cancer is very aggressive, it responses well to Chemo, with about a 75 to 80% chance of putting it remission. The bad news was, when it came back, the Chemo would not be as effective.

Prior to Bonnie's scan, Camp Quality had their bowling party, with Bonnie taking a pass to get some rest. So Shelly and I went, and Shelly was having ball, although not bowling much, she did the arts and crafts with volunteers. While I was sitting there, a volunteer came up and we started talking, well, I started, telling her Shelly's history, and the latest development with Bonnie. Shelly came running up and said that she wanted to buy Nana and me frogs for our anniversary. Already having a frog, compliments of Shirley, I said I didn't think that was a good idea. But Shelly persisted. The volunteer asked where to get frogs, and Shelly said at Petsmart. The volunteer said "I'll go with you and help you pick them out."

"Ixnay on the rogsfay!" I said in my best 'pig latin', sliding my hand back and forth under my neck. We didn't need more frogs. Shelly insisted. Knowing Shelly wouldn't relent, I cut a deal with her. I said that if she would eat a good, complete meal on Monday, then Tuesday after school we would go and buy one. She agreed.

Monday came, and we had one of Shelly's favorites, Salisbury steak. She ate two patties, mashed potatoes, and peas. Dang, looks like we'll be buying frogs. The next day came, and off we went. Petsmart had no frogs, or at least we didn't see any. BUT, they did have toads. A whole aquarium full of fire belly toads. Shelly said "Here's some!", not really reading the sign.

I saw an out. I said, "Shelly, these are toads. You said frogs, and they don't have any."

"These will do Papa, we can get these for you and Nana." So I found a clerk and requested two toads. Shelly said "We need and aquarium for them" as I wondered where that volunteer was, as I sure needed her wallet. The clerk took us to the aquarium section, and pointed out some in the $100 to $150 price range. I said, show us something smaller, which she did, but then said we needed something for the toads to get out of the water, as they do not stay submerged like frogs. Boy, a Biology lesson along with my purchase. You can't beat that. So we picked out a ceramic bridge for the toads. I could see the clerk figuring out her commission already.

"What do toads eat?" I asked.

"Oh, they only eat live crickets"

I wondered, do they take plastic here? "OK, do you have live crickets?"

She probably thought I would never ask. "Sure, over here, do you want small ones at ten cents apiece, or large, at eleven cents apiece?"

Hey, what do I know about the eating habits of toads? "Give me the large, a dozen"

It got better for the clerk, (who was thinking about retiring on her commission), she asked "Do you have any cricket food?" as I stifled a laugh.

Boy, she had me hook, line, and sinker. Playing along, I commented "No, ran out last week". I don't think she caught it. "What do you recommend?"

She said "Well, we have dry food for them, but then you have to see that they have water, or we have this small jar of orange chunks that have water in them, so you don't need to add water". I could sense the rest of the store staff was wetting their chops, thinking they were going to have a record breaking month in sales.

"OK, I'll take the orange chunks", wanting to make a mad dash for the door before she sold me a service contract. "How much are the chunks?" I had to ask.

"That jar is only $8.95" as I sized it up, about the size of a tomato soup can.

We took it home, and set it up, "Happy Anniversary Honey" I said, "Cancel the cruise."

Dr. Lois Teston wanted a CT scan of Bonnie's head, to see if it had spread to that area. She has given Bonnie plenty of pain killers, and hopefully this would help her get back to her old self (no pun intended), as she already mentioned another cruise. With the limited time, I hoped Bonnie was capable of a dozen cruises, but that was positive wishing.

Dr. Teston decided to give Bonnie one quick dose of Chemotherapy, at a reduced dosage, instead of the normal three day daily dose specified for the prescribed protocol. That one dose was so poisonous to her body that it almost did Bonnie in.

People told me that God never gives a person more than they can handle, citing 1Corinthians 10:13. But I don't believe that is the case. Some theologians argue that God gave us free will, by 'original sin' in the Garden of Eden, and that when we are over-whelmed, and just can't cope, that he gave us Jesus to lean on, and help us through these trying times. Whatever is right, and I'm no theologian, I needed help, support, anything to ease my pain, and help me help my girls to fight off their cancers.

A few nights later, we found Bonnie twice on the bathroom floor, and had a major struggle to get her up. She was in severe pain and at times, incoherent. We called the doctor, and were told to take her the the ER at UH in Cleveland, as the doctors there are familiar with her, and that she would probably be admitted. I graciously declined because of the distance we would have to travel. It was different with Shelly, as we felt we had no option. But with an ER 5 minutes away, it was a no brainer. There, they performed the CT scan and the results showed that the cancer had metastasized to her brain. We agreed to have her admitted to Akron General, and I would talk the next day with the doctors. We needed to get a better picture of Bonnie's prognosis, and if we should subject her to anymore painful Chemotherapy. It was a decision I did not look forward to, and I prayed that God would help me with the decision.

The doctors ordered more tests for Bonnie. Instead of the 6 months to a year that we were told about prior to her Chemo, they were talking about weeks. Bonnie's calcium level was elevated, an indication that the cancer was progressing rapidly. Additionally, her kidney enzyme was up, an indication that her kidneys were failing. I canceled an MRI scheduled for her brain, what was the use. The cancer has already spread to her brain. Any treatment would not help, so why subject her to any more pain. They decided that she should be moved to Hospice. Bonnie was at peace with dying, knowing that Jesus was waiting for her and that she would be pain free. I didn't know what else to do.

Bonnie was transferred to Hospice on Ridgewood, and loved it there. The staff had remembered us from 2 years earlier, when Bonnie's mother was there for 4-1/2 months. It was a peaceful and serene setting, with a bird feeder just outside her window. Shelly, not understanding the true ramification of Hospice, was excited, because the pond in the back was stocked with giant 4" Bluegills, and she remembered fishing there when Great Grandma Woods was there. She took her rod and Barbie reel, and planned on catching a bucket full. We planned a fish fry, and invited everybody (tongue in cheek).

Bonnie was drugged up, felt very little pain, but amazingly, she was quite lucid, and had been talking to all of her visitors. I had called her sister in Georgia, who called her son, Steven in Florida, and they made plans to come up.

But Bonnie continued to get better. Apparently it was the Chemo that almost killed her. She had a good day as she walked down to Shelly's fish pond with Shelly's Oncologist, Dr. Cooke, and his assistant, Linda. They were as amazed as the rest of us. But she may have overdone it, as she was in pain overnight, complaining about her breastbone, and not being able to get comfortable. She was having good days and bad ones. The Hospice doctor, Dr. John Petrus, said that he would evaluated Bonnie to see if she could be released home, and be monitored by the Home Care staff.

The next day she felt even better, and said she wanted 'Barberton' Chicken. For local people in and around Barberton, there are four (used to be five) restaurants that serve chicken dinners. These dinners are complemented with French fries, Cole slaw, and what they call 'hot sauce', which is like a Spanish rice, but made with peppers. The city supposedly sells more chicken dinners per capita then anywhere else in the country; consequently, they bill themselves as the 'Chicken Dinner capital of the world.' So off I went, returning with a bucket of chicken with all the fixin's. As we sat around Bonnie's room, munching chicken with a handful of family and friends, laughing, and joking, Bonnie's sister walked in, with son Steven and his wife Sally in tow. I think Elaine was upset, not seeing her sister dying or on her death bed. We told her that Bonnie may be released to go home soon, which compounded her frustration. "What's going on?" she wanted to know.

They stayed for three days, Elaine having the philosophy of any more than three days mice and visitors wore out their welcome. Elaine's son Steve, during that time, did a lot of yard work for me, hauling and starting to level dirt that I had delivered for a base to a new swimming pool we purchased for Shelly.

I was apprehensive about Bonnie coming home, although I knew she wanted to come, I did not know if I would be able to care for her adequately at home, especially her pain management. I ached for Bonnie, knowing she wanted to come home, and Lord knows I wanted her home too, but I'm wasn't sure if that was the best thing. I prayed that I would make the right decision when it came to that. I, no we, meaning almost everybody, was struggling with the quickness of events. Even though Bonnie seems at peace with dying, she asked me nightly, "Am I going to die tonight?" I tried to assure her that I didn't think so, but if she did it was OK, that Jesus was waiting for her.

By the middle of June Bonnie was at home, and starting to feel better. We discussed with the visiting Hospice nurse, and ended up with Dr. Petrus, about the course of action. He said that he rarely recommends it, but he felt Bonnie should go off Hospice care and resume treatment. We agreed, and an appointment was set up.

I took Bonnie to Dr. Petrus' office, as she (we) had many questions that we needed answered. Not that we got that many answered, but the doctor was surprised at how good she looked. To which Bonnie quipped "Gee, maybe I should have wore make up!" People that knew Bonnie knew that was typical. He ordered new blood tests and a chest X-ray to get a feel as to how the cancer has progressed. He stated that when he last saw her, he felt she only had a few days left. Boy, (thankfully) she proved him wrong. He stated that without treatment (based on poor blood results), she has only weeks left. He feels that the Chemo she got poisoned her, and almost killed her, causing her to be hospitalized. So this time around, if her blood results are good, she will get a modified Chemo treatment, maybe even an oral medication. The results showed a definite improvement in her blood chemistry, so he wanted to go with the chemo.

Back to Dr. Petrus' office for an out patient infusion, then a visit with him. He said he was going to give Bonnie three days of chemo. I got upset, and asked him if he knew that she had started a three day regiment with Dr. Teston, and that's what put her in the hospital. "Oh," he said, "I wasn't aware of that".

"Did you read her file!" I demanded, "It's in there, did you read it?"

He paused, then read her file while we sat there. He then stated "I gave her a 'reduced' amount, I didn't think that she could take a full amount".

Well hello! "Dr. Teston also gave her a reduced amount, and only one day of it. Are you going to give her a full three days?" I was hot. I'm not saying he was incompetent, far from it, but he was either lazy, or overloaded with patients. I wasn't going to let him arbitrarily go on and treat Bonnie without being aware of her history. That boarded on incompetency.

More reading on his part, then he said "I think that one treatment should be all that she gets. Come back in a week."

Bonnie didn't improve, but she didn't get worse, either. We returned the next week, and Dr. Petrus said that he wanted her to get the other days of chemo treatment.

Just when things were going fairly well, we had an about face. My mother was released from Copley Health Center, and went to my brother's house, where he and his wife Geri would take good care of her. However, the day after bringing her home, my brother had chest pains, and the ambulance took him to the hospital with what could have been a heart attack. The doctor said it wasn't, but he had some blockage in his small arteries, and that it would be treated with medication. Terry (Shelly called him the 'You drive me nuts guy') would be coming home the following Sunday, in time for his granddaughter's graduation party. I asked people if there was room on their prayer list for another Thornton, to please add Terry, or the 'You drive me nuts guy!'

My brother did have a minor heart attack, according to his doctor, but was still released with instructions to change his diet and get some exercise (yea, fat chance, but maybe his only chance).

Meanwhile, Shelly had returned to her old self. Full of energy, wanting to do everything. I took her to one of three parks daily. Of the three parks, one had a small playground, with not too many kids. One was a large, open playground, with walkers, basketball players, tennis courts, and lots of kids. Her favorite, and mine, was the third one, Ft. Island/Griffins Park, which had a enclosed playground with plenty of things to play with. On the occasion that nobody was there to play with, I would play tag, or as Shelly called it 'Tag-you're It' and chase each other around until I would collapse from exhaustion. (Have you chased a seven year-old around lately?). While there I befriended a wonderful lady, Belinda Thomas, who, naturally fell for Shelly. She just happened to teach high school at the same school my niece, Kim, was teaching. Belinda had her two kids come and play with Shelly occasionally. Her kids, Kara, a tall, big, pretty 13 year old girl, and Jared, a twelve year old boy. Usually Kara came, and Shelly insisted on playing leap frog with Kara, and then other kids would join in. It was quite a sight. Kara would go over Shell without any problem. But Shelly would have to literally climb onto Kara's back and work her way over. Belinda and I would just crackup. It was so funny, even Kara was laughing, but Shelly was determined to get over, and continue the game. She wasn't doing it for laughs, she wanted to play leap frog. It was moments like that that will forever be in my heart.

July came, and so did Camp Quality, with Shelly back at full speed, and as a camp veteran, she was ready. She had the same companion, Kelly, and they hit the deck a-running, or at least Shelly did. Once again she buddied up with her two best camp friends, Boo (real name Caitlyn), and Madison. Of course there were others she hung around with, but it was usually those three together. At this camp the three picked up Dominique and Kimery, and often the five would have their pictures taken together. In anticipation of some of the campers not making it to their high school prom, the camp once again had their yearly prom. As had been the case, it was a blast, with all the girls dressed in formals, and the guys decked out in tuxedos. We (Bonnie and I) were a surprise invite, because of Nana's condition, and we were able to see first hand the good times the kids had. Shelly was so tickled to see us!

While Shelly was at camp, Bonnie stated that she wanted to go on one last vacation. We discussed our options, and ruled out a cruise. It was just too much activity, too much walking, and dealing with flights, ingress and egress to the ship. We decided to go to Niagara Falls, since we all had passports, and it was only a four hour drive. I made motel reservations.

We had another birthday party for Shell, and because Bonnie wasn't able to help, I solicited, via Caringbridge for volunteers. Talk about all the wonderful people out there, they came with food and muscle to make the birthday party a success. And they came bearing gifts, making Shelly very happy.

We left shortly after the party for Niagara Falls, and stayed on the Canadian side, which we always did. We took a borrowed wheelchair for Bonnie. Unfortunately the sidewalks in Niagara Falls Canada were as bumpy as in the Bahamas, so Bonnie got juggled around a lot, no matter how carefully I tried to push her. Shelly enjoyed the arcade, and showed Papa that she did have some skills on the Miniature Golf course, beating me by two strokes. I think she's prepping for the Women's PGA. There are three 'spook' houses along the 'strip', and Shelly wanted to go in one, but backed out at the last moment. On the last day there she said "let's do it!" and so I walked her down Clifford Hill to one of the houses that had 3 levels of 'spooking'. I talked to the attendant, not wanting Shelly to come out crying, but wanting her to experience it, and the attendant said that their level 1 was just the thing for little ones. They have a series of small lights throughout the dark hallways to inform the staff what kind of 'spooking' is requested. We went through, and Shelly came out triumphant, and very proud of herself. We went back to the Motel and Shelly went swimming with her mother, while I stayed with Bonnie. We left the next morning, and had no complications going home.

After returning home, we received a call from the UH Oncology Clinic with the results of Shelly's latest scans, and all of which were GOOD! We had just finished them, but Linda, who is Dr. Cooke's PA likes to give us good news, and not kept us waiting. Shelly and I celebrated the completion of the tests by going to the Children's Museum at University Circle, which is a wonderful hands on place for smaller children. Shelly had a good time, and I had to drag her away to leave.

Shelly was doing much better, and full of energy. As if we didn't have enough things going on, Shelly wanted to take, or go to gymnastics. How could I say 'No'? Another bucket list item? Who knows, so off Shelly and I go, down to the local Pinnacle gymnastics center. We met with a very pleasant, young lady, Amy Alexander, whose eyes light up when she smiles. I explained Shelly's condition to her, and asked about enrolling her, either in a class, or individual instructions (which would be more costly, but for how long?). I said "let's go with the individual instructions", not knowing how regular we could be with all that was going on.

Amy, such a wonderful person, said "OK, there will be no charge" and immediately took Shelly to the leotard rack and had her pick out one which she also 'comped'. Already Shelly had worked her magic. Amy loved Shelly so much that she called Thursdays thereafter 'Shelly Thursdays', when she knew Shelly was coming. She taught Shelly personally. I still could not get over the love and affection that people, strangers, showered on Shelly.

Bonnie was still struggling with her Cancer, and was in some pain, but mostly just tired and fatigued (is that the same?). She ached, knowing that if she didn't continue with chemo she would not be around for Shelly, unfortunately the way she was, she wasn't interacting much with her anyway. I hoped that she would come back to how she was before the last Chemo so she could have some quality time.

We received more good news from Bonnie's doctor. The last Chemo treatment had reduced her tumor that was causing most of her pain by 75% of it's original size. No further Chemo would be necessary at that time. Now, all Bonnie had to do was get stronger, and fight off the affects of the Chemo poisoning. The good news was that she didn't have to go back to see him for a month, with the next CT scan scheduled for November. The bad news was, further Chemo would not eliminate the cancer, as it had spread to other parts of her body. We were aware that the cancer was terminal, but she was holding it at bay for the time being. I prayed that she got her strength back so she could have the quality time with Shelly that she so coveted.

We went home, thinking, November? November? Isn't that the six months that Dr. Teston said that she would have. What just happened? Did he know something and wasn't telling us, or was he just 'blowing us off?' It didn't make sense. We were perplexed.

Our friend Susie contacted the Beacon Journal, Jewell Cardwell specifically, to see if she could arrange a Goodyear Blimp ride for Bonnie and Shelly. Well, Jewell pulled a few strings, and it was arranged. Shelly could even take her BFF Josey with her. Bonnie, Ajay and girls, and, with room for one more I relinquished my seat so Susie could go. They went up for about an hour ride, and they even let Shelly steer it. She put the nose down at about a 45 degree angle before the pilot took over the controls, much to everyone's pleasure (except maybe Shelly's). Needless to say, the next day the Beacon Journal had pictures of the flyers and a very nice article about Shelly and Bonnie.

Susie was talking to her neighbor about Shelly, showing the neighbor pictures from the Beacon Journal of the blimp ride. The neighbor said "I saw this little girl. She was coming out of Strictland's in Montrose with a pink frozen custard, and told this old man 'I don't like this, I want a white one!' To which the (mean) old man said, 'But that's what you wanted, you'll not get another one'. My husband was going to offer to buy her one, as we were sitting there eating ours with our daughter, but my (adult) daughter said 'Don't butt in Dad', so he didn't".

That was Shelly, getting love from complete strangers, but where's the love for the (mean) old man?! I mean, give me a break, Shelly 'wowed' them at camp, and at her birthday party. I think we've created a (loveable) monster.

Going back to school went something like this, I think. Day 1: Shelly woke up at 4:30 and wanted to go. Day 2: She didn't want to go! Claimed Josey and Nicholas weren't in her class (but she does get to ride with them on the bus). She also decided that she wanted to take her lunch (5 minutes before the bus). After waking everybody up in the house, she goes off to the bus stop with her lunch (she ate 2 bites of her sandwich at lunch, claiming she didn't have enough time). Day 3: Went off without a hitch, and no lunch (Friday is pizza day). We got through this (at least Shelly did).

Now, on the lighter side, Shelly and Ajay were riding with me coming back from the store when Shelly asked "where do we get our money?" "I mean, you don't work, Mommy doesn't work, Nana doesn't work, I don't work!" Now, I didn't have many talks with first graders, so I didn't know if Shelly was 'typical' (I should have known that she was not), but it seemed rather astute for Shelly to notice that money comes from working. I hoped that she would keep this insight as she became an adult.

I explained to her that I worked for 45 years, and that each year I put some money back to live on, as did the government on my behalf, and now they are giving it back to me. It's called Social Security." You get it when you are retired"

"Oh", Shelly said, so you are "retarded!" I laughed, and Ajay lost it.

We returned home Sunday from a great weekend at the Kalahari Water Park in Sandusky. Shelly had a wonderful time, and was especially happy when Nana was able to get in the hot tub with her. Although Nana (Bonnie) was exhausted when we got home, she, like Ajay and myself really appreciated the work and contribution that the Camp Quality people put into the weekend. I use to think that the Quality referred to the program, but I now know that it refers to the staff of this great organization.

Back to Bonnie: I took Bonnie to Dr. Teston to get another opinion. Not that we were dissatisfied with Dr. Petrus, but we felt that he should have been more proactive than he was advocating. Dr. Teston reviewed Bonnie's history, and answered our questions, and felt that if Bonnie was willing to go through more pain with another round of Chemo, than that's what she should do.

Bonnie stated 'Let's go for it', wanting more time with Shelly. She was hopeful to get through Christmas, so more scans were scheduled and another round of Chemo (again at a reduced dose) later in September. Hopefully we would be able to take another mini-vacation, which was still in the planning stage.

We had a busy week, with Bonnie getting another round of Chemo, and Shelly having surgery to remove her Mediport and her G-tube on that same day of Bonnie's chemo. We hoped that this milestone would not have to be repeated for Shelly, but that was the case in December 2010 when she also had them removed.

Just when I thought I couldn't be more proud of Shelly, she outdid herself. Maybe it was typical of her age, and hopefully her generation. She said that she talked in her class about her cancer, and Nana's cancer. Then, she showed her class her 'G-tube' and her Mediport, that was going to be removed that very day. Not only that, she asked the surgeon if she could have her Mediport and G-tube for show and tell when she went back to school. Maybe it was just me, but I was very proud of the way she was handling her cancer, and I truly believed that she would beat it, because she wouldn't stop fighting. She had recovered nicely from her Mediport and G-Tube surgery and was eager to get back to gymnastics.

Bonnie was getting weaker, and was in a lot of pain. We wanted her to get stronger after her chemo. We talked about having Christmas early, to make sure Bonnie could enjoy Shelly's visit from Santa. Jewell Cardwell called and asked if we would be interested in the Polar Express (again). That was a 'no-brainer', the question being 'How many seats will we need?'

Bonnie's Chemo was put on hold. Because of her recent falling and confusion, the doctor wanted a MRI of her brain, thinking that the cancer has messed her equilibrium. If that was the case, then she wanted to give Bonnie radiation instead of Chemo. She emphasized that it was not a cure. She sent us to another hospital system, the Cleveland Clinic, which had a radiation treatment center close by in Medina. Boy, the insurance company must be going nuts, Akron General, UH Hospitals, the Cleveland Clinic. I guess it's time for a little payback, because insurance companies seem to call all the shots anyway. Little did I know, but I would be receiving bills a year later, so I guess it wasn't much payback.

Because of Shelly's surgery and Bonnie's expected Chemo being on the same day, Susie accompanied Bonnie and our son Steve to the Oncologist. Shelly's good friend (used to be Bonnie's) Shirley accompanied Ajay, Shelly and myself to Rainbow for her surgery, which went extremely well. The doctor said to keep her home tomorrow, but Shelly keeps pushing to go to school. When we got home from Cleveland, I took Bonnie back to UH's Clinic. When we got home from that, Bonnie crashed and slept soundly. The results of her scans last week show the cancer had spread to her liver, lungs, spine, and hip.

We had a small victory. My bride of 47 years got up out of bed and walked by herself to the bathroom. Like I say, it was a small victory, but if you have been visiting recently, you knew how weak she was, and had required help sitting up and getting up and walking. She had completed her 10 rounds of radiation, and it has helped with the pain. Hopefully, it would help her get stronger. We would just have to wait and see. The doctor has talked about more Chemo, but Bonnie seemed (as did the rest of us) reluctant to go that route. Chemo really made her sick and weak. The reason why she walked by herself was because Ajay and I were napping. It was hard to be 100% all the time.

Many people provided meals for us. My brother and his wife, Terry and Geri supplied a Bob Evans meal. My cousin JoAnn and her husband Ted also supplied Bob Evans and Red Lobster gift cards. Apparently my family remembered what a bad cook I was. There were others, many others, too many to try to mention, because I know I would forget someone. Meals came from parents of Shelly's school mates, from neighbors, from friends, from people from Camp Quality. All of which were opening their hearts to us.

On the lighter side in early October, Shelly went with our former neighbor and went kayaking with Polly (another bucket list check). She took along her fishing gear (a real sportsman she was), but didn't catch anything. It couldn't have been the corn that she was using as bait.

Shelly was such a trip. She said to me "Papa, the lights on the toe of my right Sketcher doesn't light up! Let's go buy another shoe".

When I explained that you don't buy shoes one at a time, she then said "Well, let's buy two, then we will have a spare!"

At the end of September I had a hard decision to make, but with the encouragement of many others, I decided to go to my 50th Class Reunion. Susie and Mugginhead (Ralph) brought a meal and sat with Bonnie and Shelly, helped Ajay, along with Christine, who came up from Mansfield to help, while I went to the class reunion. Bonnie was in a lot of pain, and the doctor had taken a CT scan of her back, and decided to give her radiation on the back to ease the pain there, along with treatment for her brain and hip.

I sort of remembered where the reunion was, but when I got there, there was nobody there but OLD people. Thinking I was in the wrong place, I started to leave when I heard someone yell "Hey Thornton!" Wow! Imagine, someone at this party with the same name as me! I turned around to see who this person was, when this old man came up and shook my hand. He then identified himself as a childhood friend that I haven't seen in 50 years. I guess I had a senior moment. The reunion went well, with a lot of people that I hadn't seen for a long time and enjoyed catching up with. I hope I didn't dampen their fun with my story of Shelly and Bonnie.

It also gave me a glimpse of retirement as it could be: talking of golfing, travel, cottages in the woods for the summer, Condos in Florida in the winter. Would I trade my life with them? No, I can't give up my girls, nor can I wish upon them the nightmare that I was living. Did I wish things differently? Of course. I prayed for a cure, for no pain, for fun times. But only God can ease the pain. We, (really Bonnie and Shelly) would continue the fight.

Shelly loved her Nana, and everyday before school, she gave Nana a kiss and hug goodbye. The love between these two always brought a tear to my eyes. I hoped when my time came that she would do the same for me. We took her to see Dr. Cooke for a routine checkup, but we never knew, with the nightmare of the previous December always on our mind.

We got the results back from Shelly's visit to Dr. Cooke. All her counts were NORMAL. All of them! We had never had all her counts be normal. Now, that was not to say Shelly was 'Normal'. Anybody that knew her knew that she was anything but normal. She was bouncing off the walls at the clinic, waiting for Dr. Cooke. Once again he exclaimed "Look at her. She looks great!" I'm glad he aced his course in Med School on visual observation, otherwise I'd be worried. Next up would be a complete set of scans in the coming November. We're a little apprehensive, recalling last November her scans were all negative, but then in December she had the tumor on the brain. We prayed for no repeat of that.

Bonnie was slow to recover from the radiation, eating little, and sleeping a lot. I prayed that it wasn't all for naught, but she needed to get her strength back. She had already decided that she did not want more Chemo, and we supported her in her decision. It would have been great if she got her strength back to celebrate Christmas with Shelly, but that seemed like a long way off.

Well, Friday the 13th came on Thursday that October of 2011. Bonnie was very unstable and weak that morning, unable to stand or walk on her own. Her oncologist told us to take her to the ER for evaluation. She was diagnosed with Pneumonia, and had to be hospitalized. Akron General had no open beds! Her doctor's hospital, UH in Cleveland had no open beds, but said they would give her a bed in the ER until one opened up, so an ambulance took her. I drove up, and as of 9 PM that night she still didn't have a bed, but they said she would be getting one overnight, so I came home to take the girls up the next day.

Shelly had cried when she couldn't ride in the ambulance with Nana, nor would I allow her to go to a large hospital ER room that night, so she accepted going the next day. It was going to be so hard on her to lose Nana.

We had good news and bad news. The good news was that Bonnie didn't have pneumonia, and that there is no additional treatment that she would get. The bad news was that she was released to Hospice, where she was before. The doctors say that if she got stronger, and could support herself, she could be released home with Hospice Home Care. It seemed like a long shot, but I took it. Shelly went on a sleep over at Josey's. She was really excited (about the sleepover). Shelly comforted Nana by giving her a teddy bear that she slept with (Bear-Bear) and gives lots of love to. I hoped Bonnie would get stronger and come home for Christmas. We talked about celebrating Christmas shortly after Halloween. We were hoping to pull that off.

Shelly changed her mind and didn't want to sleep at Josey's. Said she wanted to sleep with Nana at Hospice. God, I loved that little girl.

Bonnie was getting worse as her time with us came to an end. Her pain had increased so Hospice started giving her morphine. She slept all the time and could not verbalize. It was so painful to see her go through this. She has lost almost all of her hair and was uncomfortable all the time. I prayed that the Lord would take her soon to end her pain. I prayed that He would give us strength to get through this, especially Shelly, who would really miss her Nana. Her school family, from the Principal down to the families of her classmates had been very supportive, and I really appreciated them. As did I appreciate all the loving and caring friends and family that had come to visit and help us get through this, if it was possible to get through.

Bonnie earned her angel wings on, Saturday Oct. 22, at 9:54 PM. She was in very little pain, and passed in her sleep. I was with her at the time, and she passed peacefully. Unfortunately, the rest of the family were not able to be with Bonnie when she went to heaven. Ten years after I predicted that we would be 'Easy Street', Bonnie died, and the road ahead doesn't look to rosey.

with Mommy

with Mugginhead

Eight

AFTER BONNIE

It was hard to go forward. I, we, missed Nana a great deal. But it was on the little things that it showed up. Coming back from the Camp Quality Halloween party three days after her burial I was thinking of telling her what Shelly did, but then I realized she wasn't here. Rolling over in bed and reaching for her, she wasn't there. Calling her and asking if she wanted me to bring home sandwiches, she was not there. It was hard. Very hard. Shelly was struggling, especially when she didn't get her way, but it was understandable. We just had to work through it. I contacted Dr. Laura of Akron Children's to help us get through it, hoping some counseling would be helpful.

Shelly started another cycle of scans, with one on Thursday in early November, and more on Tuesday through Thursday of the following week. On Wednesday night of the second week, Shelly complained of a bad headache, and I really missed Bonnie helping me decide what to do. Ajay had stayed in Cleveland overnight with some friends, so I wondered if we were going to have a repeat of last year. I talked to Ajay on the phone and she told me it was the SSKI medicine Shelly takes to protect her thyroid from the radioactive MIBG that causes the headaches. I was still scared. I gave her Tylenol, and she went to bed at 8 PM and was OK the next morning.

Shortly thereafter, as we were leaving Rainbow, a TV interview was being taped of Shelly's favorite surgeon, Dr. Ed Barksdale. Shelly, never one to be stopped by an interview in progress sign, walked up and gave Dr. Barksdale a hug (you gotta love this girl). Well, guess who was asked to be in the interview (I mean, she charms strangers just by walking by them). So, I was promised to be notified by e-mail when the piece would be on, and who knew, the section with Shelly could be edited out, but I wouldn't bet on it. Unfortunately,

I was never notified, and we found out after the fact that it was on Christmas Day, in the morning, which is really a slow TV time. A friend who viewed the show asked us if it was rehearsed, because if flowed so well. That was Shelly for you.

We completed Shelly's scans, and knew we would get (formal) results the following Tuesday, upon our visit with Dr. Cooke. However, just when you think maybe things would start to become normal, some scans had extra things being done. Linda, Dr. Cooke's assistant didn't call with preliminary results, so we began to wonder. It appeared that there was an indication that showed up from the MRI that was located where her tumor on the brain was last year. Now the doctors aren't saying it's cancer, because they want to see the results of the MIBG scans which would highlight the cancer locations, so we waited to see. But, even if it's not cancer, it is something that must be dealt with, so we weren't out of the woods yet (if we would ever be).

The following Tuesday we had our appointment with Dr. Cooke, who told us Shelly's cancer was back. It was in many locations, but not in her brain.

I didn't know what to do! The pain was overwhelming! This little girl deserved so much to live, and there wasn't one damn thing I could do to insure that. I was mad, but I didn't know who to be mad at. I prayed "PLEASE GOD, HELP SHELLY!" She was upset, thinking she would not be able to go on the Polar Express. I didn't know where to turn. Everyone was saying "What can I do to help?" How could I tell anyone what to do when I didn't even know what to do myself? How do I maintain some semblance of order, how do I answer Shelly when she asks for another stuffed animal? We already have two large bags of stuffed animals that she doesn't play with for 'Toys for Tots'. How am I able to go on? One step at a time, one day at a time just didn't cut it for me. Had God deserted Shelly?

Dr. Cooke called with an interim report. He said her counts were good, but her bone marrow results showed Neuroblastoma present. He said he reached out to Dr. Mosse at CHOP for her input, and had not heard back from her. He intended to talk with former colleagues at UM (Michigan) for their input.

I was perplexed. After all, it was Shelly's body. Should I be telling her that with no treatment she would be seeing Jesus, Nana, and Great Grandma and Grandpa Woods? That WAS one of the options. But subjecting her to potential pain and anguish if she were to end up there anyway should a 7 year old have a say? Maybe I was being fatalistic, but I want her as long as I possible, I guess I was selfish that way, but I loved this little girl sooo much that I didn't know what to do from one day to the next.

Of course on the day we were getting ready to go on the Polar Express, Shelly was very excited. I was also excited for her. The following day she would be going to a gift making/wrapping party of Camp Quality. I 'reached out' through CaringBridge to truly thank all the people for their words of encouragement, the meals, the gifts, but most of all for their prayers for my family. It was a very hard road to travel, but knowing the Lord and many, many friends and family were traveling it with us was a big help. CaringBridge was a wonderful site that enabled us to communicate with all that wanted to know about Shelly's progress.

On Friday, before we went on the Polar Express, she conned 3 or 4 people out of dollars for the crane machine at Max and Erma's, and then proceeded to extract 4 stuffed animals from same (as did her friend Josey), hey, like she really needed four more stuffed animals. Then, on the Polar Express, she conned Joey, Josey's mom into buying her things at the gift shop. (Papa also got conned). I always though Shelly had said she wanted to be a Rock and Roll Star when she grew up, and but had since thought more about being a Veterinarian or Doctor. Personally, I thought she would be either a Con-Artist or an expert pickpocket.

On Saturday at the Camp Quality gift wrapping and making party, she picked out her 'mark', Karan, the Butterfly Kisses Photographer, and gave her some lovin', (hey, who can refuse lovin' from a blonde, blue eyed beauty?), and then, to soften her up, got picture ornaments taken with her. Karan gave Shelly a big Hershey's candy bar. Shelly then asked, "Can I go home with you?" (The mark was like putty in her hands).

"Of Course!" Karan replied. "After we eat we will go see the Christmas tree lights on the square in Medina." With the hook firmly in, Shelly finally returned home with a second Hershey's candy bar and another stuffed animal, this time a horse about half as big as Shelly.

The day before Thanksgiving Shelly asked "Papa, will I ever be a normal girl?"

With tears in my eyes, and love in my heart, I replied "Normal? You're anything but Normal! You're special! How many kids can go into a store and have complete strangers buy them presents? Or strangers wanting to buy them ice dream when a mean old man won't buy you another one. You call that normal? You will never be normal! I only hope and pray that you will fight off this cancer, and that I live long enough to walk you down the aisle and dance at your wedding." God, I loved these moments with Shelly.

Shelly really had a flair for style, wanting her red head band with the red rose to wear for Thanksgiving. I guess she gets her clothes awareness from her flamboyant grandfather. Alright, I guess I'm only semi-boring in my taste for clothes. Fortunately, Nana's taste wore off on Shelly. She ate well at Thanksgiving dinner, and really enjoyed the pineapple upside down cake brought by Uncle Steven. The meal was far from being a disaster, with Cousin Rick saying everything tasted the same. Of course I didn't have deviled eggs, marshmallow sweet potatoes, ham or scalloped potatoes, but what I did manage turned out OK.

On a more serious note, Dr. Cooke had contacted CHOP, and they felt that the best course of action would be the high level radiation, MIBG, that she had received before. Unfortunately, they couldn't accommodate us until the week after Christmas, and Dr. Cooke, along with his colleagues, felt that we shouldn't wait that long. He was going to contact Cincinnati and see if they could perform the MIBG sooner. Regardless, Shelly would be getting a port put back in, probably a Broviac, the following week, hopefully by Dr. Barksdale. We were waiting a call back from CHOP to discuss what port she should have, and talk about other options. We were presently in a holding pattern.

I've been very wrong about what I saw as Shelly's future. She was not going to be a pickpocket or a con-artist. She was going to be an artist (move over Michaelangelo, DaVinci, Grandma Moses -Grandma Moses???), I mean, she had her painting (if felt tip qualifies as a painting) 'Butterfly and Rainbow' sell at auction for -$1100.00 at the Ed Bear fund raiser the Monday after Thanksgiving.

We were still waiting for feedback from CHOP, but after talking to Dr. Cooke the previous night, he said that they felt she should get the MIBG (high radiation) treatment (at CHOP). Still, he hadn't received any feedback from Cincinnati or UM Medical Center. Everything was still on hold, so we were trying to be patient, but it was hard when your little girl had cancer spreading through her while we waited.

To paraphrase Robert Frost, "but I've decisions to make, and miles to go before I sleep, and miles to go before I sleep." Shelly was scheduled to have her Mediport surgically reinstalled the first week in December. Discussions with CHOP and Cincinnati Children's Hospital Medical Center helped define the options, but no definitive direction to go, outside of probably going with the MIBG treatment, which both hospitals had.

CHOP could perform the procedure the week after Christmas, but recommended 5 days of Chemo prior to coming, then retaking the scans the week of the 19th. The downside was, the Chemo Shelly would get, she had had before, and it made her very sick, so she would have to be admitted for the procedure.

If we went to Cincinnati, they would perform the MIBG prior to the 15th, as the manufacturer shuts down for the holidays at that time, and MIBG had a very short half-life. Another consideration was that Cincy's protocol had a lifetime limit of 50 millicuries/kg, and Shelly had used up 36 already during her prior two treatments at CHOP. So she would only be getting 14 this time. This limit was dictated by the FDA, and could not be deviated from. The doctor at Cincy, Dr. Weiss, who actually wrote the Protocol that is used and regulated by the FDA, was not sure that a third round of MIBG at a reduced dose would be effective, as there was not enough data to make a value judgment. Regardless, he felt that if she could get 18 at CHOP, that it would be more effective than what they could give her at Cincy. He suggested that this be verified first, as CHOP was working on an experimental basis, which would not be regulated by the FDA. He suggested that maybe a new protocol of Chemotherapy, followed by a Stem cell transplant may be the route to go. This would use up her last bag of stem cells harvested three and a half years ago at Akron Children's Hospital.

It's scary, knowing that we would not have any more (stem cells), but they may have to be used for the MIBG treatment anyway, so we wait to see which way we go. I was getting more and more frightened, and prayed that God would help us and the medical team to make the right decision for Shelly.

As was to be expected, Shelly's surgery to install a Mediport went well, if you call getting up at 4:30 a good thing. After coming home and resting (well, I'm not sure Shelly rested, but I sure did), we had Susie and Ralph come over (at Shelly's insistence), and they brought pizza. After pizza, and a few games, Shelly had a sword fight with (Sir) Ralph and then did X-Box (by herself). You just couldn't keep her down. I guess that really made me a bad parent - oh, by the way, we went to Malley's chocolate store in the afternoon. Shelly's 'boredom time index' was about 2 minutes, as she always had to be doing something.

We had talked to the doctor before we left Rainbow, and he was still waiting to hear back from CHOP about the qualification of Shelly for the full dose of MIBG (18 milirems/kg vs. 14). That being the case, we would be going to CHOP after Christmas. Shelly is having a hard time with this, thinking that she wouldn't be home for Christmas, again, but we were hopeful that she understood that we were going after the Holidays. In preparation for the MIBG at CHOP, she would get 5 doses of Chemo. She would not be able to resume her gymnastics until 12/19, as she really enjoyed that.

Boy! Talk about your non-stereotypical doctors, Dr. Cooke breaks the mold. Dr. Cooke called on the weekend, and told me that CHOP does not have a lifetime limit on their MIBG, so we are going to Philly the week after Christmas. Shelly started her Chemo at Rainbow for 5 days. Depending on her reaction, and the time it takes, she could possibly be going to school after each dose.

We ran out of luck. After the first two treatments went well, but slowly, Shelly developed a low grade temperature (100.8 F). I gave her Tylenol, and called Dr. Cooke. He asked us to go to Rainbow Babies ER, for she might have an infection, which showed up negative - is that an oxymoron? Well, since we were already in Cleveland, and it was after 10 PM, they admitted her to Rainbow 2 (the Oncology floor), because she would be getting another dose of Chemo the following day. It turned out that the hospital also had a 24 hour rule for fever admissions, so we had to stay another night (only), providing everything went well on Thursday with the Chemo. Ajay wanted to stay Thursday night, but I would rather go home and sleep in my own bed and come back on Friday, but that was contingent upon Shelly being able to come home on Thursday.

We were talking about going to a swimathon and then to a Birthday party and sleepover. Shelly's school principal called and asked about her going to 'shop with a cop'. But her headaches persisted, and, would not go away, so we stopped Shelly's social activities. After her Chemo treatments, they took a CT scan. We received more bad news. The indication that was in the same location as the tumor last year and had grown since the scans a month ago. She would have to have an MRI to help define the tumor, and it had to be reviewed by the neurosurgeons. Shelly was always very good with all the procedures, from CAT scans, to X-Rays, to MRI's, although the latter were least liked by her. She would lay for some of the scans, without moving, for up to 60 minutes. But for the MRI's, not only did she have to lay still, she was subjected to the loud, associated booming noise. After finishing her MRI, the technician said that they had to do it again. Shelly got very upset. She was crying, but, after Ajay gave the tech a piece of her mind, she calmed Shell down and she went through it again.

We left, and was hurrying to Shelly's school, where Christopher Milo was putting on a performance, and we all wanted to be there. As we approached the school, I received a call from the MRI people, stating they needed another one, and wanted us to return to the hospital. Boy, talk about being upset. I told them that we would return after the concert, or come back tomorrow, but we were not going to miss Christopher's concert. They said they understood, and told us to come back after the concert, which we did. None of us were happy campers. We met with them afterward, and decided the best course of action was to put off the trip and treatment at CHOP. It did not look good, with the doctors putting her on steroids to diminish the swelling that caused her headaches. But it did not appear that a cure was in the forecast (if it ever was). They were talking about comfort, and quality of life, which I didn't want to hear, because these are the same words I heard for Bonnie, and she didn't get much of either. I know Nana fought it with Chemo and radiation, and got nowhere. I didn't know if or what we should do. We really needed Divine intervention. I knew God loved Shelly, and He wanted her, and that He was going to take her, but I wanted to keep her as long as I could. "Please God, make Shelly's pain go away AND let her grow up to be whatever she wants" I prayed.

Shelly's first grade teacher, Mrs. Ann Rochford, came to visit bearing gifts (I gave up saying anything). Among the gifts were four giant cards signed by each of the classes (K - 3) at Hillcrest Elementary School. Over 400 signatures from her classmates and friends, wishing her wellness and love. Then a big envelope with cards from everyone in her room, each expressing love and happy thoughts. It was breaking my heart to come to grips with what lied ahead. We kept plugging, but, we needed God's help, we needed a miracle.

Additionally, sooo many people had reached out to us with offers of meals, cleaning, shoveling snow (not yet), and anything else. I knew everyone was sincere, and I said that from the bottom of my heart, but I didn't KNOW what to do, what to eat, where to go, or what I wanted to do. I needed help, but I didn't know what.

Shelly went to school the next day, but was very reluctant, stating the noise level was unbearable (I didn't know if that's the problem, or she just wanted to stay home from school).

We were scheduled to see the doctors, and hopefully come up with a plan (I didn't know if it would do any good, but I prayed that we would have more quality time with Shelly). We returned from the hospital after meeting with the doctors, and had more information, but no definite course of action. Dr. Cooke felt that removing the tumor on the brain would lengthen Shelly's quality of life (which may be a no brainer to some, but we had some reservations about brain surgery on Shelly). We talked with a neurologist, Dr. Gold, and she wanted us to talk to the Neurosurgeons, and would set up an appointment for us. We reviewed Shelly's medication extensively with not only Dr. Cooke, but with the Palliative care team and physician, Dr. Humphrey. They changed her meds to help with pain management and stomach aches. We still didn't know what was going to happen, or when, but we were still hoping for a Christmas at home for Shelly.

12 DAYS OF CHRISTMAS

Day 3 of the 12 days of Christmas, I didn't know it, but apparently the word got out that we celebrated 12 days of Christmas. On Wednesday, Dec. 15th, our neighbor, who was moving to New Orleans, came over and insisted on giving Shelly a present. After he made a special trip to Target for purchase, Shelly opened (an intriguing game called Mind Flex). Then yesterday, a gift card in the mail (which Shelly opened) had to be redeemed at Toys R Us. Then the staff at Ajay's favorite watering hole, The Musketeers called and said they had a gift for Shelly, so we stopped there before taking her to her class Christmas party. Lo and behold, not a gift, but 6 gifts wrapped, which she promptly opened. Then, on to school, where she received a beautiful prayer shaw. Additionally, she got another gift card to Toys R Us. Our friend Joey took Shelly and her daughter, Josey and they went shopping and got more gifts. The next day Shelly's Camp Quality companion, Kelly came bearing gifts (over my objection). Did I mention Camp Quality? Their Christmas party was Saturday, also, so gee, I wondered who would be getting gifts?

Now, people have asked me what I needed, and, I've decided that one of those large, storage containers, like they use on ships to transport cargo, placed in my front yard (maybe a heater and a

Port-a-potty) for me to live in, because there would be no room in the house for me by the time the 12th day of Christmas arrived. (I was just kidding about the Port-a-potty).

We planned to see Shelly's Oncologist, Dr. Cooke on Tuesday, Dec. 21st, and hopefully he had a plan of care for her treatment. Then on Thursday, we were to meet with the Neurosurgeon to discuss the pros and cons of brain surgery. We weren't moving as fast as we wanted in arriving at a decision. In reality we did not want anything done anyway until after the 12 Days of Christmas. Regardless, we still needed Divine intervention.

After talking to the Neurosurgeon, and 6 different doctors the next day, exhaustively we had a direction for treatment. The Neurosurgeon (Dr. Bambakotis) told us that even with surgery he would not be able to get all the tumor out, so we talked to the Radiation Oncologists, on the assumption that with radiation treatments they could get the rest. The Radiation Oncologist told us, after consulting with the Neurosurgeon that a procedure called Gamma knife surgery would get ALL the tumor, would only take one visit, was non-evasive, and could be done the following week after Christmas. The low with this, was that we had to be at the hospital at 6:30 AM, so we would be staying at the Ronald McDonald house on Wednesday night (a small price). Additionally, we would be able to start treatment for the rest of her cancer, probably at CHOP, as discussed previously, ASAP, instead of waiting 4 to 6 weeks while she recuperated.

Now, for all the cookie makers out there that were planning on making cookies for Santa, be informed, as I was, that all little kids knew Santa doesn't like Chocolate Chip cookies. See, even the little kid in me didn't know that, so make some sugar cookies for the old man, and Santa too.

The Palliative Care team assigned a young, outgoing visiting nurse to be Shelly's nurse. Angie Gruss was very conscientious and really cared for Shelly, and told us to call her anytime there was a problem. On Christmas day Shelly was in a lot of pain. We took her to the ER on Christmas night, as was suggested by Angie, who had contacted Dr. Cooke, who was visiting his mother in New Jersey for the holidays. Once in the UH hospital, getting the pain under control took some doing, but we finally got released on Wednesday. Since Shelly was scheduled for Gamma Knife surgery the following day at 6:30 AM, we decided to stay at the Ronald McDonald House. Shelly was happy with that idea.

Even during her pain at the hospital, she managed to bring happiness to many people. She had fun wearing a red 'clown' nose when the doctors came in. She also had fun with Christopher Milo, having him chase her remote control helicopter around her room and out into the hall. She received a large bag of toys from the hospital and from the Ronald McDonald House (My room addition was almost done). She brings me much joy, so, to paraphrase Christopher Milo, "Why did you, Lord, chose us to give such a special, loving, smart, witty, beautiful child?" Forget the Cancer, I would never, ever, trade my situation for anything, short of a cure for Cancer.

Shelly has brought me to tears and laughter in an instant. She said that a gift blanket reminds her of Nana. "Why?" I asked. "Because it has frogs on it, and Nana has one of our bathrooms decked out in frogs".

Then, after I made crumbs on her bed at the hospital, she accused me of being one of the 3 Stooges, you know, Larry, Curly and Dopey (her names for them). I can't tell you how much that cracked me up. As I have said before, I have 3 (now adult) older children, and, none of them made me laugh as much as this little one. Ajay would say she needed an occasional break from Shelly to be with her friends, but I believe it's actually to get away from me. But that's OK, because there was no place I would rather be than with Shelly.

Shelly had passed the Gamma Knife surgery with flying colors. In fact, the first words that she said in recovery were "Where is my sausage?" Since she could not eat before surgery, she requested of Christopher Milo, at 6:30 that morning, that she wanted McDonald's breakfast sausage. Well, needless to say, Christopher made it happen. She ate, and this was while still in recovery from brain surgery, 2 sausage patties, one pancake, and an order of scrambled eggs. That was at 2 to 3 PM on the day of surgery. We left the hospital, went to the Ronald McDonald House, where she had conned a friend of

Ajay into making his famous meatloaf for supper. Of course she was hungry (boy the steroids she was on were something), so she ate a cupcake, a brownie, and a bowl of ice cream. I'm glad they have a big refrigerator that is well stocked, because I was not sure that what we had at home was any good. Supposedly after her two helpings of meatloaf we would be going home. We were scheduled to come back the following week to clinic for counts.

After my butt fell asleep watching 23 bowl games on New Years Day, I decided to get up and do something. With the weatherman predicting up to 6" of the white stuff, I thought I would get a jump on it and shovel the 3" already accumulated. Who knew, we could get another 12". So I bundled up and got my push shovel out and started on the driveway. About 1/3 of the way through, the garage door opened, and I thought, wow, Ajay's going to help me. But no! What to my wondrous eyes did appear, but a miniature snow person all bundled up with a small shovel. "Let's get to it Papa", and this little person proceeded to pitch in. God, I loved this girl. She just warmed the cockles of my heart. I'm sorry, I'm getting mushy and poetic, and I'm not a poet. It was such a joy to finish the driveway with MY GIRL.

The first week of January we went to the hospital for counts and to start another round of Chemotherapy (5 days). Over the Holiday weekend we had a little trouble with pain management, but kept it under control with the help of the Palliative care team and Dr. Cooke. Her counts were low, so Shelly received a bag of platelets, but no Chemo. We went home, but returned two days later for an ultrasound of her abdomen, because her liver enzymes were low. Hopefully we would start Chemo the following week. We juggled her meds (at least her doctors did), and she was not in pain, but still was eating like a horse. She continued to eat the leftover pork and sauerkraut that was brought by the mother of one of Shelly's classmates.

Because Shelly felt that she was not pulling her weigh shoveling the snow, she asked if we could go to the store and get her a bigger shovel, or a maybe a small snowblower. (You had to love how this little girl thinks). Well, I nixed the snowblower, but bought her a small shovel. After a trip to the grocery store for Mega soup and ice cream, to Petsmart for crickets to feed the toads, to Circle K for Lawson's Chip Dip, and to 5 Below for crazy straws, we got gas for my snowblower and came home. Shelly was starving, the steroids had kicked in full time.

Christopher and his kids, Tally and Nick, both really great kids, joined us at our favorite Barberton Chicken house. Afterward we came back to the house to watch WWF Smackdown. Prior to that, the kids were flying Shelly's remote control helicopter and her air swimmer, Sharkey. Of course Shelly had to finish her Chicken Parmesan that was left over from the Olive Garden. If you're confused, you should have been here trying to keep up with her eating.

Who knows what the next day would bring, both health and menu wise for our little girl. Shelly has gained 6 pounds since she's been on steroids (she's wasn't so little, but she was still my little girl). Shelly's Chemo had been pushed back until she had completely recovered from the Gamma knife surgery. We went to the hospital for an Ultrasound of her abdomen, to see if something was going on there. The Ultrasound came back normal, but her platelet count was still low. Dr. Egler, the resident specialist on Neuroblastoma who worked with Dr. Cooke, said it was probably taking her liver longer to come back because of all the trauma her bone marrow has gone through. When her enzymes were in an acceptable range (maybe with additional platelet transfusions) then the Chemo treatment would begin again. In the meantime, we were juggling doses of her meds, as the new one, Periactin, made her zombie like most of the time. When she was awake, she was eating. Nothing had stopped the steroids. The following morning she had French toast, sausage, grits for breakfast. She followed that up with fried chicken, French fries, and Cole slaw, which were leftover from the chicken house. Then, she had ice cream, and chips and dip (all before 11 o'clock – in the morning!).

She received platelets and would go back for a doctor's visit and a CT scan of her abdomen. The following week (if you're wondering, the week of Jan. 16, so much was happening so fast) she would go to UH for a MIBG injection on Tuesday and subsequent scans on

Wednesday and Thursday. Christopher Milo said he would meet us tomorrow at UH, so Shelly promised to bring her remote control helicopter so he could run up and down the hall chasing it. We were still trying to get a handle on the pain, and continued to juggle her meds. She had to have her platelets at a certain level and her liver enzymes as well before we could go to CHOP for MIBG treatment, which was still an option, but we didn't know when.

Shelly was disappointed that we didn't have any more snow so that she could use her new shovel. Do childhood labor laws apply to kids with cancer? I didn't think so, so I would use her.

Well the beat went on. Just when we thought we could catch our breath, we got hit in the gut. We couldn't get Shelly's pain under control on Sunday, continually increasing the amount of meds, trying other prescribed meds, then calling the visiting nurse. Angie came to the house and gave suggestions. Nothing seemed to work, so off to the hospital we went at 10:15 PM. They admitted her, and, after some placebos, Shelly was pain free, or too tired to care at 1:00 AM in the morning, so she fell asleep. I did also, even though those couches weren't the best for old bones, or at least not mine. After talking to the doctors, her meds were juggled some more and off we went to the Olive Garden, where she had her chicken Parmesan, and enough leftovers for another 2 meals, which would be gone by breakfast, before we went back to UH for her MIBG injection.

Believe it or not, but Shelly actually asked for MY meatloaf, which I would prepare. I think that was another bucket list item for Shell.

Just as we finished supper our power went out. As I said "Looks like I won't be able to do the dishes", I got a beacon of light from Shelly. There stands Shelly with a flashlight and a battery powered lantern. "Here you go Papa, what did you do, forget to pay the electric bill?"

"Not this time" to the laughter of Ajay and Uncle Steve. Only Shell. In the dark we went for gas and then to Strictland's for frozen custard (vanilla for Shell, Butter Pecan for me, a sundae for Ajay - Uncle Steve left, he had come to play cards with us, and it's sort of boring sitting around in the dark trying to play cards, so we didn't).

Unfortunately, Shelly's pain came back, and we called the nurse, who contacted Drs. Cooke and Humphrey for their input. After 3 doses of Dilaulid, one of Periactin, her Melatonin, and a Tylenol 2 (with codeine), I think we finally got her pain under control. Hopefully she would sleep through the night.

We went to the hospital to complete Shelly's MIBG scans, and to get counts. We received good news! Her platelet count was up to 72 from 66 at last count. This showed her little body was making platelets on their own. Plus, her liver enzymes were down to 142 from 1400. This was a good number, qualifying her for treatment at CHOP. YAHOO!

We were weening her off of steroids, so her weigh should start dropping soon (and her wild mood swings). I missed my high energy little girl, and I prayed that she got back to normal soon. Plus, her doctors changed her meds, so maybe she would be in less pain.

Just as we thought things were settling down, Shelly said she couldn't see out of her right eye. Although she gained her vision back shortly thereafter, it was blurred. A phone call to the nurse led to a return call from Dr. Cooke, who was quite concerned, and wanted us to come up to UH's ER. So off we went. After the ER docs examined her, a call went to the Ophthalmologist. Upon examining her, the doctor said she would like an MRI of Shelly's head, as her right eye was dilated more than the left. We were admitted to Rainbow 2, and, after some doing on Saturday, Shelly got an MRI, and the results showed no abnormalities, so we went home. Shelly went to see a concert at Akron's E.J. Thomas hall with Christopher, his kids, and Ajay. They also went bowling on Sunday, so it's been a busy weekend for Shelly. It seemed she never slowed down.

Shelly had some pain, but the pain management was under better control. We went to see Dr. Cooke, and hopefully he had reached out to CHOP and we would have a date firmed up to go there. Shelly had a low grade fever on Monday, January 23, so we called the doctors, which led us to the UH's clinic. By the time we got there, her temperature was normal, but she got counts and antibiotics anyway. Ever more important was the info Dr. Cooke gave us about going to CHOP. It would happen the following week, with the arrival day not yet firmed up, but they wanted us there on Thursday.

We went to Philadelphia for treatment. We spent the first two nights at the Sheraton, compliments of the good people at CHOP or Ronald McDonald's. That's where a dilemma came in. On checking out, the Concierge, a nice lady named LaToya Jones - I would think that a 'Concierge' would be named Jacques, or Bridgette, or a French name. So this nice lady asks me, how was your room? This is where the dilemma came in: The room was 'comped', so do I have a right to comment? I mean, I was taught to never look a gift horse in the mouth. Should I tell her that the bottom bed sheet wasn't tucked in? That the top sheet was tucked in, but there was an additional four feet of sheet at the top that folded down? Does she really care? After all, I was 'comped', so I shouldn't be complaining. I replied, "It was fine" Anyway, I got that off my chest, it was really bothering me.

Well, we got back from Philly late, and, although admission to CHOP was slow, everything went well and her decompression time was only 2 days. Since only one family member was allowed in with Shelly at a time, as there was only one dosimeter, Ajay and I rotated days, with me being there the first and third day. On the third day, Shelly said she wanted to talk to her mother, and asked me to call her. I said I would, but that she couldn't touch my phone, because she was still radiating 'zoomies'. Well, Shelly said, why don't I wear the rubber gloves that you're supposed to wear when I hold the phone, that way the phone won't get contaminated and we won't have to throw it away. Outside of the shot she took at me, it made sense, so I called her mother and let her talk to her.

We will be seeing the UH doctors soon, and based on the scans to be taken in 6 to 8 weeks, what the next course of action would be.

Shelly's counts were good on Tuesday, and we will be going locally to get counts on Friday, only going to Rainbow if blood/ platelets are needed. She will be going to UH on Tuesdays for counts. Her scans to determine how well the MIBG (that's short for, here it goes, Methiodobenzeguandodine) got the Neuroblastoma will happen in 6 weeks from treatment. Hopefully she will keep her counts up in the meantime, but the doctors at CHOP say that she should be coming back for a second round of MIBG thereafter, regardless. They think the second round will eliminate the cancer. Shelly hopefully will return to school next Monday (2/13), although she will be getting counts on Tuesdays at UH, and Fridays locally.

Shelly has some problems with pain, so Tuesday her medication was adjusted, and we kept her home from school the rest of the week, and, hopefully she would go to school the following week.

Well, our normal Friday visit to the UH clinic started on Thursday, with Shelly having a fever of 100.6 F, which isn't that high, but the doctors were concerned that she had an infection, with a very weakened immune system. She had been diagnosed with a Urinary Track Infection from cultures taken on Tuesday, and we started antibiotics on Thursday afternoon.

Of we go, around 8:30, Shelly and I, with Ajay staying home as she didn't have any connections at the Ronald McDonald House for her to stay. So, as we are motoring up I-77, with some degree of urgency, I encounter a person going 65 in the fast lane - I won't say what sex she was, as I have too many female followers, and Hell has no fury like a woman. Anyway, this person wouldn't get over so that I could safely pass on the left, per law, so I passed on the right - she was talking on the phone, surprise, surprise. Well, another few miles down the road I encounter another one - it must be the thing to go out on the interstate and talk while in the fast lane. I got jammed up with other traffic, so I slowed down to 70, and what to my wondrous eyes did appear, no, not Santa, but a State Police officer waiting for speeders, of which I wasn't one at that time. I guess I owe her a "Thank You", but it still irritates me that people (of all sexes) that think they should help the police by going the speed limit in the fast lane.

After going through the ER, Shelly went to Rainbow Two. For those of you that know Shelly, you know that she is a loving, caring, funny, high energy sweetheart, and I'm not just saying that because she's mine. But on Thursday, from the time the tutor got to our home, until she finally got to sleep at 2 AM on Friday in the hospital, she was not the best child you would ever want to find. I mean, she wouldn't eat, she was yelling, crying, throwing things, well, you get the idea. They gave her platelets in the middle of the night, and then she received blood in the afternoon, as her counts were low, and she also received antibiotics for the UTI. She still wasn't eating, and wanted to go to the Red Lobster for the Ultimate Feast. I knew she wouldn't eat much of it, but Ajay said she would pay for it and split it with her.

I had many good times with Shelly, but of late they have been limited to playing video games, or watching videos from our extensive video collection. As her pain continued to increase, and we struggled with controlling it, she wanted to do less and less. I would take her to a near by park that had a couple hills for sled riding. Most of the time, we, Shelly and I would go down together, and, as time progressed, I would end up pulling the sled back up the hill, which is as to be expected, but most of the time Shelly would want to ride on it. This old man wore out easily, but I did my best. Sometimes other children would ride down with Shelly, and they would bring the sled back up, and Shelly would walk. Her mother was usually off doing her own thing. I wanted to be with Shelly as much as possible. I guess I felt that we were losing her bit by bit.

We would go down to the local video exchange, where they dealt with used videos and games, and Shelly would make her selections, and this was sometimes four or five times a week, so it became rather expensive. As par for the course, one of the managers fell for Shelly, and if he was working, would 'comp' one or two videos. When the store next door folded, and the video game exchange expanded, we kidded that it would be called Shelly's Wing, because she was buying videos regularly, and there were very few Disney videos that she didn't have.

By February 24th we finally made it to our normal Friday visit to the clinic on Friday (vs. the previous week when we went on Thursday to the ER). On the way there we had a lively, albeit friendly, disagreement about the color of an automobile, a purple car that the girls said was blue. I mean, come on, I know the difference between purple and blue, and the car was definitely purple. After we cooled down, and another car color discussion, Shelly exclaimed "Papa, you have some serious issues". I mean, those of you that know me, do I have serious issues?!!

We had intended for Shelly to go back to school the following week, as she had missed a lot, but, the doctor told us that with her counts bottomed out (whatever that means), that it would not be good for her to be around a lot of snotty nosed kids.

Shelly did get platelets that day, and a shot to boost her white blood count. CHOP advised that she should be OK without a stem cell transfusion at this time, providing she only needed to get platelets no more than twice a week, as she only had the one bag of stem cells left, and that (they are hoping) should be used as a rescue after the next MIBG treatment in Philly, probably around the 1st of April.

It is a major concern for us as I didn't know what other course of action we can take after her stem cells are gone.

Christopher, Uncle Steve and cousin Rick came over for Prime Rib on the last day of February, and, although Shelly did not eat, she enjoyed play time with Christopher, playing Wii, and flying helicopters. After they left, Shelly had a persistent (low grade) fever that would not go away (100.4 F), so we called the doctor and he told us to bring her into the ER at UH (again). In prepping her for the ER, (applying Elmo -Emla - cream), Shelly had her shirt off, and said "Look Papa! Boobies" Well I don't know about other 7 year olds (and I don't want to know), but my little girl does not have 'boobies', and I told her "You don't have boobies, you're only 7, you won't be getting them until your 13 or so, and, at that time you had better not be showing them to any boy or man, do you understand!" She laughed and ran to her mother to get the cream put on. I was definitely not ready for that.

Well, off we went to the ER, Shelly and me, and she was admitted. The doctors feared an infection or a virus of some sort, so they put her on antibiotics and took cultures to see if they could get a handle on her fever. After getting platelets, and red blood cells the next day, plus ongoing antibiotics, they could not find the source, but she no longer had a fever and was in a lot better spirits so they released us around one o'clock, on a Saturday. Shelly ate very little while she was there, so they prescribed some potassium. They said that they may have to put a tube through her nose for supplements, if she didn't start eating. Although her weight was up because of the steroids, they were concerned about her stomach not being able to process food, so she needed to eat, which was no easy task to accomplish.

On Tuesday (3/12), Wednesday and Thursday, she got an MIBG injection, an MRI scan, and two MIBG scans, all at Rainbow. If the results were positive (in a good sense, not a medical sense, I know, it was so confusing) then we would be going back to Philly for another treatment the following Tuesday, with a treatment on Thursday. If the results were bad (negative in a good sense, see what I mean by confusing), then another course of action would have to be decided by the doctors and us. Her counts were still low, and she received platelets, but her liver enzymes were normal and her potassium was acceptable. I still didn't know what it all meant.

On Saturday before we were to leave for Philadelphia, Shelly was in a frumpy mood and even a visit from the neighbor with her two boys didn't help. Because of that, and her counts being so low, we were reluctant to go to a spaghetti dinner, a 'Hugs and Bugs' fund raiser, requested by Christopher Milo. Now, I had other reasons for not going, but, we went, thinking if things went south, so would we. Well, once we found the church, and Christopher, things really perked up. Shelly ate some meatballs, garlic bread and a little salad. She also met a new friend, 4 year old Ava, who has A.L.L., leukemia, who was also in sort of a frump. After eating, a very aggressive game of 'Duck, Duck, Goose' took place, with the girls and others, including young men of 'FiGi', a fraternity from Akron U (whoops, it's 'The University of Akron' now - it was Akron U when I went back in the 30's, but I digressed) who put on the dinner. Seeing these two little girls run around was worth the price of admission, and especially getting them out of their frumps.

We got the green light to go to Philly around the middle of April for our second round of MIBG (this time), leaving Tuesday. The scans had showed that the first round of treatment was effective, with the cancer being diminished. Shelly still had cancer at a number of places, but with another treatment and a stem cell transplant subsequent to that, she hopefully would be in remission. We will still had to wait for the scans 6-8 weeks out to verify. I knew that there would be other treatment, because it was never that simple.

I couldn't wait to get my little girl back, nor could her mother, as those that have been in contact with her of late would testify. To say that she had been a bear lately is an understatement, as her cheerful, fun, pleasant personality went south, and took her manners with it. Who could blame her? I knew she was in a lot of pain, and nothing seemed to help.

On Wednesday, after having to check in at the Sheraton in Philly, we went to be admitted (well, get Shelly admitted), and did not get a bed until 7 PM. This trip Christopher Milo join us for two nights, as he had a previous engagement on Thursday and needed to return to Akron on Thursday morn. He supplied some much needed relief to catering to the Princess. I stayed overnight with Shelly. A catheter was placed early Thursday morning, before her MIBG treatment at 1:00 PM. She was not a happy camper, to say the least. The Nuclear technician came and checked out her room, which had been paper lined and covered with plastic.

Shelly got her treatment, and her initial reading was 39.1 Microcuries on the Geiger Counter. Her reading had to be under 7 before they could release her to go home. With a half life of approximately 1 day for Iodine 131, it looked like we would not go home until Sunday. Her reading on Friday was 19.1, so we made arrangements to stay at the Sheraton for two more days, having given up on the Ronald McDonald House. But lo and behold, on Saturday, her reading was 6.7 so they cut us loose after they took a baseline scan. We hit the road, and stopped at only two rest areas trying to get Shelly to eat something. She only would eat meatballs in the hospital, the only thing that stayed down, so it was OK. The CHOP doctors wanted her counts done on the following Monday, so off we went to Rainbow.

Dr. Cooke had left a message on our answering machine, so we called him and brought him up to date, and made arrangements for our Monday visit. We spent most of Monday at the UH clinic, with Shelly getting platelets, red blood cells, and a shot of Neulasta (?), isn't that a coffee sweetener? They said it was a two week growth stimulant, but I wondered. To encourage us to extend our visit, there was a power outage in the eastern part of Cleveland. Now all hospitals have emergency backups, but apparently they do not go into all examining rooms. Ajay was very upset because she had to walk down 6 flights of steps (why are steps called flights, or am I just being old fashioned?) to use her cell phone. Strange though, she rode the elevator back up, as the elevators apparently only went up during a power outage. We were scheduled to return to clinic for counts on the following Thursday, and a transfusion of antibodies to help her fight potential infections until her counts got back to normal.

It seemed that all we were doing was shuttling to the hospital, trying, hoping desperately to get our little girl back. The following week she would be admitted for a PICC line to be installed, to accommodate her stem cell transplant. In the mean time, we went to the Red Lobster for Uncle Steve's birthday, and Shelly insisted on wearing a prom dress (at least that's what she called her fancy dresses, because she might be wearing it to Camp Quality's prom), and put on a Princess tiara, and off we went. Now, I don't know if it's a female thing, or just Shelly's personality, but when I was a young lad, around 4 years old, I wore a cowboy outfit with chaps, side pistol, and hat out once. That's all I remember, and that was the last time, ever, for me to wear anything that was flamboyant. Of course I was a shy, introverted type of child, and Shelly was anything but. She so tickled me with the things she did, I loved this little girl so much. But, as with any other child, she had that dark side, being demanding, having her own way, and being quite a handful at times (but like I said, so are other kids, but at my age, she wore me down more often, or sooner that when I was in my prime 40 years ago - gee, it seemed like only yesterday).

We arrived at Rainbow Hospital the following Monday evening around 7, knowing that Shelly would be getting a PICC line installed early Tuesday for receiving her stem cells in the afternoon. I became a LITTLE skeptical when a nurse, a resident doctor, and the attending doctor asked ME what her schedule was. Hello people, shouldn't that be my question? Well, the resident found out and told me that early Tuesday meant noon in Pediatric Sedation, with the placement of her PICC line at 1 PM. I guess the whole staff was still on Hawaii time. Forgive me for sounding cynical, but we probably could have come to the hospital on Tuesday morning, but it was OK, as long as it got done (you see, I've mellowed in my old age). After getting a medicine faux pas straightened out, which involved 3 doctors, our local pharmacy, and myself, off Shelly went to the Sedation unit, with Mommy, Christopher and me. Shelly was sort of in a frump, but Christopher and his Donald Duck routine, plus his doctors hair cover quickly got her laughing. The PICC line was inserted on the inside of her left bicep, with the line going (internally) up her arm and over to near her heart. I have lost count of the number of minor surgeries that Shelly had been through. In fact, I wasn't sure of the number of major surgeries that she had, knowing that I just wanted her healthy, but that approaching dark cloud continued to get darker, and closer.

After her PICC line surgery, she returned to Rainbow Two, where she and Christopher were flying helicopters awaiting for her stem cells. Although this was her third and last bag of cells, I don't remember witnessing her receiving them before. She had 15 million cells available (with only a minimum of 2.5 million needed - why they weren't further divided was beyond me), and were inserted with a large hypodermic needle directly into her PICC line by Dr. Cooke's able assistant, Linda Cabral. The stem cells looked like a cherry slush, and each hypo took 8 to 10 minutes for insertion. Shelly got sick during this transfusion, which was not uncommon, but orange Popsicles helped get rid of the bad taste created in her mouth. When the procedure was done, she received 3 hours of fluids, and then we were released. Shelly did assist the resident with removing her PICC line (well, actually the tape, which was the most irritating part), carefully pulling the tape over a 15 minute period. Shelly asked for the PICC line for show and tell at school. We returned home, but not before stopping at Arby's for a couple of sandwiches for Shelly. Shelly was eager to see her cat Smokey, and insisted that he sleep with us (She removed him in the middle of the night). We talked to Dr. Cooke, and would see him in clinic on the following Friday. Our next milestone would be the scans in 6 weeks to determine if the MIBG treatment was successful again.

Just when we thought things were getting better, we went to Appleby's for lunch, courtesy of Cousin Rick. Shelly took a bite of her shrimp and a couple bites of French fries, and told her Mom she needed to go to the restroom. Just before the door, she lost her meal, and her discharge contained a substantial amount of blood.

When we got home, her temperature was only 99.9 F, so we cleaned her up, and her clothes, and called the doctor. They wanted her in the hospital, like immediately and said she would be fast tracked through the ER, so off we went. You know things aren't going well when you are on a first name basis with the hospital security guard. After getting platelets again, and red blood (is it any other color?), and being observed overnight, we were released, but not before Jason from Camp Quality showed up as Whinny the Pooh. He was a treat for Shelly, and all the other children he encountered.

Well, just when things were settling down, we got off the roller coaster and got on the Tilt-a-Whirl. As we were getting ready to go to the U of A Songfest fund raiser for Camp Quality, Shelly got sick and had diarrhea. To compound the problem, her stool was almost black, and her emmesis also had black in it. Since our effort to get a hold of Dr. Cooke was futile (his phone was dead), we called the visiting nurse who said that dark discharge is indicative of 'old' blood, and that the addition of Vitamin K as a medicine was to help her blood coagulate. This information put our minds at ease, at least a little, since Shelly's still wasn't eating, or keeping anything down (with blood in her stomach, I can understand).

Dr. Cooke finally got hold of us, and told us that her numbers are really coming back, and that he's pleased with that, but is perplexed about the blood in the stomach, which could be the result of an ulcer. Gee, like Shelly hasn't had enough problems. He planned on seeing her Tuesday in the clinic, even though he's on rounds in Rainbow.

The doctors were concerned about Shelly's G-I issues, and had a G-I doctor examine her. He wanted to scope her (Upper tract) to see if she has anything going on, like possibly an ulcer. This little girl didn't get many breaks. She was admitted and, what is normally an outpatient procedure, would be two to three days for her, as the doctor wanted her 'loaded-up' with platelets before and after the procedure. So off we went with Ajay getting the first shift, as I had a doctors appointment the following morning.

Dr. Cooke eliminated some of her medicines, and hopefully, she would start getting better. Angie visited us in the clinic, and observed how different Shelly was than on her home turf, giving everybody a hard time, even Lucilla, her favorite and regular nurse. I guess she was fed up with the whole hospital routine.

After threatening everybody in recovery for slipping in a catheter (forgive the pun) during her leproscopy to get a clean urine sample, Shelly settled down with a warm, comforting bath, after which she was almost human. That night she actually ate some pizza. Her counts and attitude were so good that they sent us home. Results of the scoping showed a potential ulcer, but not yet, so additional medication was specified to coat her stomach prior to eating. She insisted that we go to Olive Garden, so off we went, with Shelly eating salad and about a 1/3 of a chicken Parmesan patty, which at that time was a lot for her.

Shelly went back to school, at least for half days. Shelly was still having 'attitude' problems (maybe it was just me being cantankerous), but we really needed her to get back in school so she didn't have to repeat first grade. The staff at Hillcrest had been very supportive and leaned over backwards to help her.

Depression. It doesn't always come at you like the gale force winds but sometimes as a gentle summer breeze. You suddenly don't want to get out of bed, let alone actually do something. It's strange, you feel like, "Why bother?" especially when things are going wrong, and you can't cope, like with simple changes to Shelly's medication. I didn't know if I was really depressed, or if Shelly was, because it's not like a telegram that arrives and says "Hey! You're depressed". So, was I depressed? Regardless, this wasn't about me, so I asked people to say a prayer for Shelly to get her well and in remission so she could be that fun little girl that we all knew and loved. Her scans to evaluated the success of her treatment in Philly would take place Tuesday, 5/08 through Thursday 5/10 (Nana's birthday – God, did I miss her).

Shelly, unlike me who has friends in lowly places (can you hear Garth singing?), has friends in highly (higher? up there? well, you get the idea) places. Shelly and I were invited to see the Cleveland Indians from a suite. We not only had free parking, but a buffet that included hot dogs, hamburgs, chicken strips, hot wings, sub sandwiches, a veggie tray and a fruit tray, to say nothing of peanuts and cracker jacks ("I can hear you singing now - Buy me some peanuts and..."). As the weather was a balmy 40 F + with a breeze blowing in off of Lake Erie, we chose to stay inside and watch the game through the window, or on the High-Def TV. Shelly was a little 'bummed out' that no other kids came (because of previous commitments), but warmed up to a young couple, and got excited when Slider, the Indians Mascot, showed up with gifts for her. We stayed the whole game, and Shelly said she would do it again. We gave a big THANK YOU to the Higgins family for the invite.

Shelly went to school (reluctantly) with a headache, but we wanted her to try to tough it out, if she could. It was hard to differentiate between her anxiety and pain, and understanding what she wanted to do, not necessarily what we wanted her to do. She wanted to go to gymnastics after school, so we played it by ear. Her scans were scheduled the following week, so we waited with baited breathe.

Shelly was back in school, (rode the bus two days in a row), and continued to get tired, so she only went a half of day. The staff at Hillcrest was great. They even talk to me (I know it's hard to believe, but there are some people who don't talk to me). Shelly went on a field trip yesterday to a play at the Magic Theater, in Barberton (very creative name, being in the Magic city), and said she fell asleep during the play (it must not have been too exciting). Christopher Milo and Ajay went to her school to have lunch with her.

We, (I say we, my team, the doctors in Oncology and the ones in Palliative care, they are on my team, along with the nurses and the pharmacist) weened Shelly from her Fentanyl patches, stepping down with dose and adding supplemental Dilaudid. Shelly was still very aggressive, demanding, controlling, and generally a pain in the aa... 'elbow'. Hopefully when she's off the patches her true personality will be back, and prayerfully her scans next week will be negative.

We went to MY favorite fish place to eat on a Friday, (you know what Shelly's is), as I like their fish, and it's all-you-can-eat, or as some clever person put it on the chalk board (very sophisticated) AYCE fish. When I was naive, I thought it was acey fish, whatever that is, some kind of fish that I haven't heard of, but I liked it, so I didn't really care. When the waitress asked me "Do you want more fish Sir?", to which Shelly responded "His name is Papa!" God, how I love this little girl - although I'm not offended when people call me Sir, but just a little uncomfortable. Also, I thought 'Papa' was a title or position, not a name, but what do I know.

When we got home, Ajay gave Shelly a bath, because she didn't want to miss 'WWE SMACK DOWN' at 8 PM. During the bath Shelly exclaimed "Mommy, i got hair on my tweeter!" Now for those of you not from around here, 'tweeter' is a matriarchal passed down anatomical word for a female's private area. After her mother stopped laughing, she told Shelly that she's only 7, and she does not have hair on her tweeter. "But you do, and so did Nana". Well, Shelly got out in time for WWE, and, one wrestler wrestled with a broken arm, twice. Boy, talk about a man of steel!

Shelly was doing better, although she still got tired about halfway through her school day, and was still not eating a lot, but she was eating. We were still waiting with baited breathe for her scan results.

On May 11, one day after Bonnie's birthday, the results, or interpretations, of the MIBG scans were in! Once again, Shelly's body responded very well to the MIBG scans. In the doctor's words, "These scans look pretty darn good!" (I don't know that he used an exclamation point, but the quote is correct). There is one caveat though. Her right arm, the humerus, had a very slight indication, faint, and hopefully with the MIBG still working, will disappear. Also, there was a 'faint' spot on her lower left rib, which hadn't shown up before, and could have been caused by incidental trauma. That's two minor issues, but only one is a caveat.

COURSE OF ACTION

Well, that's a good question. Dr. Cooke recommended to just enjoy life. He feels that no further treatment, or scans are necessary at this time. We all needed a break, and with summer coming, Kids Day at the Zoo, Kids in Flight, Camp Quality, Shelly's birthday, and who knows, maybe even Cedar Point, all this before a yet to be planned trip back to Disney in September.

FUTURE MEDICAL WORK

What are the medical experts going to be doing at this time? Well, it's not sitting on their hands, that's for sure. CHOP has requested the biopsies from Shelly's old tumors, to investigate the genetic code to see if any of their new medicines will be applicable.

with Nana

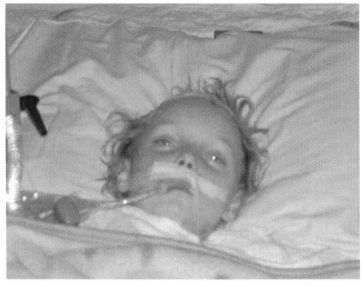

In PICU before brain surgery

Nine

PAIN FREE

At the end of May, Shelly continued to go to school, eager to finish first grade (still a half day - she needed to rest before gymnastics). We went to the clinic, and her counts were good, and she was taken off two medicines. When we got home, Shelly went to the bathroom. She called out "Papa, I went No. 2" (Now I don't remember my other 7 - almost 8 - year olds needing me when they went No. 2, but I digressed). She continued "I need some Senna".

"Why?" I asked,

"Look, nothing but little rabbit turds" she replied.

Although she was being weened from her Fentanyl patches, she still had some pain, and struggled to go to school a full day, it was probably fatigue, and not all pain. Although Monday she had a great day at gymnastics. Talk about a mixed message.

Shelly was plugging along, as were Ajay and myself, but still not eating much, so we thought about putting her back on Meggase to stimulate her appetite. Shelly was looking forward to Josey's birthday party on Sunday, and maybe going to the street carnival in Kenmore this weekend.

Shelly, in missing Nana, suggested we get another cat. I wasn't sure I saw the comparison, because Shelly already had a cat, Smokey, whom she loved dearly and who hung on her where ever she went. After much discussion, we went to the local animal shelter, and asked for a cat that was docile, as Smokey was a very passive, friendly, cat, and we wanted one that was compatible. We found 'Blackie', an all black cat that was very skittish, but we thought that was just because of being in a cage. We brought Blackie home, and Smokey attacked him, and Blackie withdrew more into himself. In fact, he disappeared, in the house, for two days (we never let our cats outside). We couldn't find him. Didn't know what to do. Then we saw him in the litter box, and hightail it behind the washing machine. As much as we tried to coax him out, he would not come. He then developed a respiratory infection, and, we felt that we could not adequately take care of him, so we returned him to the Animal shelter. At that time, Shelly feel in love with a rambunctious, high energy kitten that she absolutely had to have. So, guess what, we brought home 'Whiskers', as Shelly named him.

So we had this aggressive, playful, 2 pound kitten. Whiskers was determined to exert himself as the 'alpha' cat, or in this case, the 'alpha' kitten. Smokey could not eat without Whiskers edging him out of the way. I finally decided to put two food bowls down, thinking that they would each have a bowl, but nooo, when Smokey would start to eat from one bowl, Whiskers would come over and edge him out, causing Smokey to go to the other bowl. That didn't deter Whiskers, he would go to the other bowl and do the same thing. Smokey would finally gave up, and walked away. Later he would sneak some food while Whiskers napped.

Shelly was doing better, although her appetite was still missing. Her counts were staying stable, so Dr. Cooke spread out her regular visits to bi-weekly. Shelly would complain that, after two bites, everything tasted funny, so she was kept on Meggase.

While playing cards with Shelly one night she startled me with "Papa, please don't spank me naked!"

Not knowing what caused her to say that out of nowhere, I replied "OK, I'll keep my clothes on!" First of all, I haven't spanked Shelly for over two years, the last time being when she refused to get out of the bathtub for Nana. I told her if I had to go into the Jacuzzi to get her (out), then I was going to spank her bare bottom. Well, she dared me, (more or less) thinking Papa's never, ever spanked me before, so he's not going to do it now. Guess what? Case closed. I really wasn't sure what prompted Shelly to say that, but it's hard to be mad (at anybody) when you're laughing, and Shelly did not get spanked (for whatever reason).

Shelly went with her friend May-May and May-May's grandmother, our friend Shirley to a movie, and then to May-May's house for a sleep over. Around 11 PM on June 22, the phone rang, and I thought 'this is not good', but it was Shelly calling to say Goodnight. When I asked her if she was having fun, she started rambling (where does she get it?) about a campfire, roasting hotdogs, 'Smores and watching a movie on the neighbors garage door. Boy, I love this little girl. I reminded her that we were going to "Kids in Flight" on the following day, and that Shirley and May-May were going with us, so don't be late getting home in the morning.

'Kids in Flight' is a wonderful organization that takes seriously sick children up in small airplanes for a flight around Cleveland. It is an all volunteer organization. Additionally, they supply food on the ground along with face painting, crafts, and other activities. We were told that three of us could go up in the plane, so we invited Shirley to bring 'May-May' along.

Well after the threesome arrived in the morning and we took off, the girls had just happened to smuggle Whiskers in the car to take with us. Can you imagine my anguish when they tell me when we are about a mile from Burke Lakefront Airport that they brought the kitten (in a large purse)?

After I settled down from wanting to beat the girls to death, we went in to Burke and, believe it or not, the kitten received a warm reception. The girls and I were privileged to get to fly over Cleveland in a 4 seater Beechcraft, which was enjoyed by all.

A few days later Shelly had an MRI scan done. Preliminary reports from the scan showed the tumor has come back, or at least an indication. The Gamma knife doctor has yet to review it, but Doctor Cooke reached out to the doctors at CHOP, Rainbow's resident Neuroblastoma doctor, the doctor of Neurology, and other specialists for their opinion. There was no further treatment available at CHOP. There may be some Chemo (oral) that Shelly could use. A new specialist reviewed her scans, as did the Tumor Board. Dr. Cooke told us to go ahead with her Camp, and her Birthday party at the end of July, so the end was not imminent. It's so hard to keep up the false bravado. I know Jesus and Nana wanted her. But so did Ajay and I. I guess it was no contest. It just hurt so bad, and at times I felt like a zombie (whatever they felt like).

On the brighter side (we could always count on Shelly), when Shelly was being sedated, the doctor asked her who she had brought with her. Was this Cousin Rick that he had heard about? "No", she replied, "Just some hillbilly that was walking along the road". You have to love this girl. I guess that what made it so hard. We still didn't know what we were going to do, even as we prepared for camp and her birthday. Shelly had been eating better, for breakfast she has French toast (3/4 slice), a bowl of Fruit Loops, an ice cream sandwich, a half of bag (small) of potato chips, one and a half chicken strips with a few French fries. I guess her appetite was back.

I promised Shelly that she would not be going to the hospital during camp (next week), nor for her birthday.

On Sunday before the Fourth of July, we met with good friends Susie and Ralph (Mugginhead) and Joey and Josey at the local TGI Friday's for a meal and to view the Fairlawn fireworks. Waiting for our meals, Shelly recalled a story from when she was four. She said that she wanted her mother to have a Mexican baby. "Why?!" we asked. "So I can learn Spanish". Although it had been raining, it stopped in time for the fireworks, and we all enjoyed them, even when the police came to stop some rowdy person (not me) for shooting off a lot of them in the parking lot.

On the fourth of July, we participated in a parade for HUGS N BUGS in Stow. I have nothing against Stow, but being in the world's longest and most boring parade when it's only 97 F was a bit too much for an old fat man and almost everybody else. Shelly rode in the back of a convertible, and they eventually put the top up and turned on the air.

The day after the Fourth, Shelly was eating well, but her legs were hurting, so she passed on gymnastics and swam a little in our above ground pool. Since Ajay was going to work and out to eat later, Shelly and I went to the Olive Garden. Shelly said she wanted to go swimming again when we got home, and asked me if I would go with her. I said I would, but I would need a nap (meaning afterward, but I didn't say it or she didn't hear me) so I went to put on my swim suit, with the door closed. Shelly, thinking that I was taking my nap barged in, and saw my backside (OH, the humiliation!). She started laughing and ran down the hall screaming "Nana was right! Papa's butt is skinny and hairy!" to her mother. Now I didn't wring Nana's neck much when she was with us, but I wish I had done it an extra time for telling Shelly that.

As I was about to go to the pool, the phone rang, and it was Dr. Cooke with the latest input about Shelly. He related that a new expert examined the scan and said it MAY BE radiation Necrosis, a residual from her MIBG injection in March at CHOP. Dr. Cooke stated that we still wouldn't be able to do Anti-body therapy, as Antibody therapy did not apply to tumors in the brain, so that option was not available. As we talked about what the recommended course of action would be, this little voice speaks up, apparently Shelly had picked up another line, and said "Dr. Cooke, will I be having Gamma Knife surgery again?"

Neither Dr. Cooke nor I were aware that Shelly was on the other line, so we both got 'shocked' and had a chuckle. Dr. Cooke said the best course of action was to have fun and to enjoy herself, first with Camp Quality and then her birthday on the 28th of July. If she was still doing well, we would have more scans after that.

Later, I asked Shelly about the Gamma Knife question, because I thought it didn't hurt, being noninvasive and all. She said, if she was going to have it, she wanted to wear a hat because her head got cold.

While Shelly was at camp, Nana's sister, Elaine and her husband Bob came up from Georgia to go through her mother's things (Great Grandma Woods, who passed away in 2009). While we were talking, they reminisced about the last time Bob was here, I believed it was three years prior, and that Shelly had called him a "bad family member" because he wouldn't pass the mashed potatoes. We once again had a good laugh, but they said that they use that expression all the time back home when one of them doesn't do what they're supposed to. I took them to see Bonnie's grave, since they had not come up for the funeral. As we pulled into the cemetery, I commented that my grandfather Thornton, whom I was named after was also buried here, and that I would show them his site as well. When we got to Bonnie's site, we got out and walked over. Now, talk about slow and slower (I won't say Dumb and Dumber) Bob saw the (nice, new, shiny) headstone, and seeing 'Bonnie Sue' engraved, commented "Gee, he was married to a Bonnie Sue also (thinking this was my grandfather's tombstone).

I of course commented, 'Sure, that's Bonnie's middle name" (missing the misidentification completely). Elaine, after she stopped laughing (about 5 minutes) straightened both of us out (but it took some time). We then proceeded around the cemetery and I pointed out my grandfather's headstone.

There were times, when, seeing Shelly smile, or hearing her laugh, warmed the shackles of my heart. Now, I didn't know what the shackles of the heart were, because I thought shackles were something that inmates wore on their legs and arms. Then to warm them, I had trouble getting my old mind around that concept, let alone applying it to the heart. Anyway, Shelly continued to be in a frump, so the warm shackles were enjoyable, even though they were confusing.

Shelly and I were playing cards when we had one of these times. It was a 'Dad to daughter' moment, not 'Grandfather to granddaughter,' when she said, as she raised her finger to the ceiling, "Wait a minute, I forgot!"

Now, I was confused, but that was not unusual, I said "I can't ask what you forgot, because you just forgot it, but shouldn't that be 'I remembered'?" We both burst out laughing. I guess you had to be there, a real Kodak moment, so to speak, but my shackles are warmed when I think of that moment.

The results from the clinic visit showed her counts were very good, and her demeanor was also cheerful (receiving two presents from the hospital staff had nothing to do with it). Scans were scheduled for the week after her birthday.

Well, with scans scheduled, we threw together a quick trip to Kennywood, an amusement park outside of Pittsburgh, with Uncle Steve joining us. I had a GPS, a TomTom, and Steve had his GPS systems (phone and computer), and Ajay had hers on the phone, so the chances of us getting lost should be remote. But after blowing a car fuse, and three different routes selected, and a trip of Western PA., we extended our 2-1/2 hour trip to almost 4 hours. Anyway, we got there.

Although it was hot, around 90 F, our spirits weren't dampened, although the beer was watered down, but that wasn't what I meant (I didn't indulge, thank you). Shelly got her fill of roller coasters, but her favorite was probably the 'Raging Rapids' which she rode with her mother and me (my least favorite). To say we got wet (or at least I did) is an understatement. My shoes, socks, underwear, shorts, and shirt got drenched (even my cheeks were...well you get the idea). My wallet and phone took forever to dry out. Shelly couldn't contain her laughter, and got somewhat wet herself, but that didn't matter, because Papa 'got it good' (I know that's bad grammar). Ajay got it a little more that Shelly, but she also got a good laugh at my expense.

We left just in time for the Pittsburgh rush hour traffic (boy, I just love driving). Shelly was scheduled to go to the clinic on the following Tuesday, followed by her MIBG injection in the afternoon, and then MIBG scans on Wednesday and Thursday. She was also scheduled for a 1:00 PM injection on Friday for a MRI scan in the afternoon. It is really bad when, not just your favorite nurse knows you by sight and name, but technicians and nurses in every department, from X-Rays to CT Scans, to the Sedation Unit as well. It was a rather sad commentary on Shelly's fight. Although I think that all of them remember Shelly, and maybe some remember me.

I didn't know what to say. I felt like I ran a marathon, yet, I knew I have never ran more than a mile in my life. I received affirmation of that statement "Life isn't fair!" Boy, you got that right. Dr. Cooke had called. After all of Shelly's tests (scans), he gave me some good news. Shelly's indication in the brain had not changed, hence it was radiation Necrosis. However, her cancer had come back, or it was not completely destroyed by her MIBG treatments in Philadelphia. She showed elevated readings in her right shoulder, her lower left rib in the back, and both her thigh bones (femurs?). Because the indication in the brain was not cancer, we did not have the sense of urgency which we had experienced twice before. He, and his assistants would look into what protocols were available in other hospitals, so we might be going to Cincinnati or Michigan, or who knew where. He was talking about quality of life, and as long as Shell was cruising along, there was no rush to treatment.

It hardly seemed fair that this little, precious girl should be subjected to more surgeries than most people have in their lifetime. She had also seen doctors at Akron Children's, Cleveland Clinic, Children's Hospital of Philadelphia, Memorial Sloan Kettering in New York City, and Rainbow Babies and Children's hospitals. You know that things were serious when your doctor calls you on New Years Eve while on vacation in New Jersey. Or when a painting done by your little one goes for $1100 at auction for a charity. I prayed, "Dear Lord, please end Shelly's pain and suffering".

We had Shelly's eighth birthday party, and about 40 people showed up. Shelly's has had some pretty wild 'mood' swings, as we have had to adjust her pain medications accordingly. She was somewhat better, although she still wasn't getting much exercise, except for going to the Barberton Y for swimming, which she thoroughly enjoyed. I would take her as often as she wanted to go, or as time would permit. She continued to beat me at cards, and whipped any visitor that was willing to participate in "Jumping Monkeys".

We went school shopping at WallyWorld (aka Wall Mart) and Old Navy, where she made a new friend, the Manager, Dani, who gave her 3 tops to compliment her ensemble. It's amazing the impact this little girl had on strangers.

A few evenings later I was informed by a young lady, of 8 years of age, who shall remain nameless, that I had "serious personal issues" (again). I mean, the indignation of it all, just because I burnt her French bread pizza, I mean, come on, I also burnt mine, doesn't that count for something? After a roller coaster weekend, with the mean witch of the second grade, in which she alienated her best adult friend, her favorite waitress, and being locked in her closet for 3 days (OK, that's was a little thick, but I thought about it). Oh yea, and there was that trip to the local ER (she wasn't too friendly there, either), because she had another UTI. Boy, these medical people think we know everything, but Shelly had to tell me it was a bladder infection. With a horse pill type of antibiotic (Amoxicillin), she had recovered quite nicely, and looked forward to going back to school, which was to start soon.

We went to the UH clinic and met with Dr. Cooke, who had returned from his vacation to the Jersey shore. He outlined several options, but at the top of his list was seeing if CHOP would administer another round of high dose radiation, MIBG, which would be contingent upon harvesting Shelly's stem cells. I knew that there were many out there more than willing to offer up their stem cells, but they must come from Shelly. This was done through some premedication to enrich her blood, and then placing a 'shunt' in her groin to harvest her 'enriched' stem cells. The time table had not been established yet, as Dr. Cooke was reaching out to CHOP to get their buy in. If that could not be accomplished, then the next option would be Antibody Therapy at Memorial Sloan-Kettering in New York City. Farther down the tree, but easier pickings, were some options at UC Medical Center in Cincinnati, or at The University of Michigan in Ann Arbor.

PAIN

Pain is such a strange malady. It's amazing how much you can have in your heart when your little one has it everywhere. You wished that you could make the pain go away, but you can't. Even the doctors struggled with controlling her pain. Sometimes you just wanted to scream. But you don't, because you knew it wouldn't help. You wanted to get drunk, but that wouldn't help. You pray, but that didn't seem to help. Where to turn? Friends would say "Call me if you need help". OK, but what kind of help do I need? What kind of help will do anything?

Shelly had a bad weekend, with her going to the ER on Sunday and being admitted on Monday. She was good, and the pain seemed under control so they released us, but when we got home it was back. How do we deal with it? I don't know. Her mother was at her wit's end.

Our life was just one medical problem after another, either scans, fevers, or pain control. We were always going to see a doctor. I didn't regret it, just was frustrated that nothing was helping Shelly. We asked people to pray for strength and guidance as we fought this disease that would not go away, that continued to ravage Shelly's body. There seems to be no hope for any semblance of a normal life. That old song by Eddie Arnold "Make the World go Away" seemed very fitting.

In early September we went to the Cincinnati Children's Hospital to participate in a Level 1 study of a new approach to treating cancer (Level 1 established only dosage, and not results). We went on Sunday to be there for a 6:30 AM appointment for the doctors to do a 'workup' for establishing a current history (is that an oxymoron?). Scans would take place with us returning home later in the week. Hopefully this study, which contained some medications that have shown some degree of success would help, and lessen the pain, which Shelly continued to have. We hoped to get her back to school and a regular routine, whatever that was.

Shelly had been complaining about the pain in her right arm, that it was really bad. She said that she would like a sling. Well, I told her "They are pretty easy to make, all we needed was a scarf."

She replied "I'll get one", and went to our stash of winter scarves. When she returned, she had on a reindeer head ban, with antlers.

I commented, "that doesn't look like a scarf to me".

She replied "I couldn't find one, but I found these".

"What are you going to do with those? I doubt that they will help your arm".

"I plan to wear these to the neighbor's Christmas party" she replied. "And to the Project Ed Bear fund raiser. and I know just the dress to go with them".

I told her "it's a little early to plan on going to the neighbors Christmas party, we don't even know if they are having one, let alone if they will invite us. Let's go look in Nana's drawers, she has a lot of scarves, and I'll make you a sling".

It's these little moments of joy that were so precious to me. As we left for the next type of treatment, I couldn't help but wonder how many more would be available for Shelly, or how many more Shelly would be available (for).

I'm sure that any or all of you that have traveled with small children are familiar with the 'Are we there yet' syndrome. Well,

Shelly had a night time version of that, or at least in Cincinnati she did. We arrived in Cincinnati and had to go to bed early because we had a 6:30 AM X-ray. Shelly went right to sleep, even though she denied it. Then, around 2:30 AM she asked me, who was struggling to get to sleep, "How many hours of sleep do we have left?"

"Shell, we have 3 hours, so go back to sleep".

Then, a half hour later, "How many hours of sleep do we have left?"

At this time I'm thinking, I apparently have NO hours of sleep left, but I tried again "We have 2-1/2 hours left, so go to sleep so I can get some sleep". Yep, you guessed it, one half hour later, well you get the idea.

The next day, after a trying time at the hospital, we visited the Cincinnati Zoo, which Shelly really enjoyed, as we had spent many days at the smaller zoo in Akron, and visited the Cleveland Zoo as often as we could. We went to a large mall, and Shelly found one of her favorite stores, Claire's, where she purchased a BFF necklace set, of two plastic hearts with a 4 leaf clover in it. She said that was for luck. I asked her if she was going to give it to Josey, her BFF, and she said "No, Josey has luck, I'm going to give it to Mommy, because we need all the luck we can get".

Just when you think your little one is still naive, and wet behind the ears, she comes up with wisdom beyond her years. It brought tears to my eyes, and I replied, "We sure do, and prayers too!"

When we got home, after supper, Dr. Weiss from Cincinnati called, and said the Shelly wasn't eligible for the study, because we wanted her pain to be manageable so that she may return to school. He explained that the treatment in the study was slow acting, and that would not accomplish that. He said that he talked to Drs. Cooke and Egler at Rainbow, and said that he recommended she gets spot radiation where the cancer was causing pain. He also recommended the same 3 chemos that would have been administered at Cincinnati could be administered at Rainbow, but just not under any protocol. That sounded like a Win-Win suggestion to me.

A later phone conversation with Dr. Cooke showed he agreed with Dr. Weiss, and would start the ball rolling the next day, with all treatment being done at Rainbow. He would advise us of a consult with the Radiation Oncologist, perhaps as early as the next Friday. We would do that on our way to Kalahari for a weekend with the Camp Quality people.

We went to Kalahari, in the middle of September, and Shelly had a pretty good time. On Friday at Kalahari she did two big water slides, the wave machine, and the roller coaster with Papa (boy, I was getting too old for that stuff), and hit the hot tub too many times to count. She slept well, and Saturday, did some things with Mom to give poor old Papa a break. I wasn't poor, YET. On Sunday she went to the arcade (it used to be called the penny arcade, but now you insert your money into a machine and get a card with credits on it. About twenty dollars later, she had enough tickets to get some luminous press on nails (I mean, like wow). Then later, after going to a not worth while animal farm, that cost another thirty bucks to feed the sting rays (they weren't hungry), we went to the gift shop. Needless to say, when the clerk called me Papa, I knew I was in trouble. All in all, I would do it again, as my little girl did a lot of laughing (at my expense, of course). Unfortunately, I lost her glasses, which we reordered early the following day.

When we got home, we (actually Ajay did) gave her a bath and applied a Fentanyl patch to address the pain. She was in a very good mood, although not so much at the UH hospital where we went for a consult with the radiation Oncologist, who would be giving her high dose hot spot radiation later in the week. We came home, and she ate some Rigatoni that good friend Susie brought over earlier. Then, believe it or not, ask to go to the park, to fly her helicopter that she received for her birthday (we broke it, unfortunately), and then asked to go to another park, where we ran into our old park friends, Jared, Kara, and Belinda Thomas. It was good to see them, and even better to see Shelly in the park playing with her mother.

We visited Dr. Cooke the next day, so hopefully, her plan would come together.

Love for your child is often defined by endurance. I was coerst, volunteered, shamed (all of the above) into watching "Beverly Hills Chihuahua, 3" with Shelly. I'm not saying it was tortuous, but I would rather have had my toe nails removed, without anesthetic. I mean, even a SpongeBob marathon would be better. And then, guess what, we followed up with a two hour bout of WWE Smackdown.

Well, I guess it was all right. After all, Shelly endured her radiation treatment, about an hour and a half, without moving. The treatment wasn't painful, but the positioning and repositioning was.

She wanted me to order pizza at nine the following morning, so her appetite was back. Her low grade Chemo was started, a three week regiment as an outpatient, with three cycles of it. I didn't know what we would do after that, I was very apprehensive. Only time and prayer would tell.

We were scheduled to go to clinic on the following Friday, and probably get platelets. However, when Shelly woke up with a fever of over 101 F on Thursday we called the doctor and he told us to bring her in. He also wanted to get her pain management under control, as we had been struggling of late, so off we went. When we got to clinic, she had no fever (as usual), but they admitted her anyway for observation (and pain control).

They changed her Dilaudid dose, and increased her Fentanyl patch to 50 mcg/hr which had been restarted, and which seemed to be working. They also sent her to their dentists to check out a few cavities. The nurses on the floor (unfortunately) knew us well, and one of them asked me how Shelly was doing. I replied "She acts like a women going through the change", which caused several projectiles being thrown at me (no serious injuries, thanks for asking).

After her visit to the dentist, the Palliative Care doctor visited her to try to help with the pain management. Then, in short order, an aid came in for vitals, her lunch was delivered, two dentists came in, and the Resident and Shelly's nurse showed up. Needless to say, much to my frustration in trying to deal with all the confusion, Shelly had disappeared. Where did she go, you asked? She hid in the coat closet. I wished there had been room for me, because I had trouble dealing with everybody at one time. After the crowd dispersed, and things settled down, Shelly ate and then they took an X-ray of her abdomen to check for any bowel blockage, of which there was none. They released us in time for an Obama rally at CSU down the street, causing us to find an alternative way home to avoid the traffic mess.

Shelly was exhausted (as was I), and even said 'pass' to WWE Smackdown on Friday night and retired (went to bed, I'm actually retired) around 8 o'clock.

It was the middle of October, and Shelly had attended only three days of school, with the pain being the primary reason for not attending. We had an up and down weekend, with the new pain pump, which was attached to Shelly for better pain control, being proactive, instead of reactive. Shelly was still struggling, but had less outbursts. We went to Walsh's farm for some fall activities, of which Shelly participated in bungee jumping, of all things. She also picked out three pumpkins for carving, and some mums, of which she suggested that we place, along with a pumpkin on Nana's grave. You had to love the compassion of this child. We carved pumpkins, Shelly and I, and proudly displayed them on our front porch.

We went to the clinic the following Friday, and Shelly's counts were improving, with her platelet count up from 23 to 32 (forget about the units). She had to have it above 75 for chemo to be resumed. Because of her continuing pain in her back, and off and on pain in her head, the doctors had a CT scan of both places. Once again, positioning her arms for the spinal scan was very painful, making me wonder if it was worth all the additional pain we subject her to. On Saturday we went to Camp Quality's Halloween party, and Shelly seems in a good enough mood and the pain was moderate enough.

As we approached the anniversary of Bonnie's passing, I found myself getting depressed, but even more, getting angry with myself for lack of any initiative to do anything. Although we went to the Camp Quality party, Shelly didn't participate much in anything, nor did she interact with any of the other cancer kids that she knew well. We came home, but not before stopping at the Video Game exchange for some new videos. She then wanted KFC, which prompted a trip to the nearest one, in Medina (only a 55 minute round trip). Still feeling sorry for myself, I decided to go to bed early, when Shelly said "Hey! How about a goodnight kiss and hug?" Talk about pushing the right button. My spirits lifted immediately. I know this brief moment of joy will not get me out of the doldrums, but it was nice.

I gave her a Big kiss and hug, and said what I always say "We'll have a better day tomorrow". It's hard to stay focused on a child struggling with cancer and all of her treatments, and watching and praying that she would be getting better, but that train was going the wrong way, and I did not want to face the inevitable. I knew she was fighting, and not giving up, so I would not give up, ever. We talk about doing things, like going to Disney, and several people had reached out to us with offers, which we would gladly exercise when the time came. But at that time, we were focusing on going to her school's Halloween party/parade the next Friday, which I felt would probably be too much for her. She seemed to be managing her pain better, but her incontinence from the chemo kept her withdrawn. It was a struggle for her, and we took it day to day, so planning long distance was out of the question.

We went to the cemetery on the anniversary of Bonnie's death, taking the Mums and pumpkin. As we were leaving on the narrow roads therein, a woman, preoccupied with her grieving, came around the back of her car to right in front of us. I had seen her and had slowed down. The startled lady stepped back and got out of the way. Shelly quipped "Keep walking lady and you'll have your own stone". That's Shelly for you.

Later, we overheard the neighbor tell her son that if he wanted the car, to do his chores, to which Shelly said, "I don't have chores. Cancer kids don't do chores!" I want to talk to the person that's feeding her this bad information.

Later, I had a choice of watching (a) the Presidential debate, (b) the NL playoff baseball game, (c) Monday Night Football, or (d) a Disney movie (Atlantis) with Shelly. Guess which won hands down.

She had a very good day as her dosage on her pain pump was increased, and the pain seems better controlled. It seemed that the frequent visits by her Hospice nurse, Angie, helped with the pain control. We went to the UH clinic, and her Platelet count was up to 52 (thousand), on it's way to 75. She had to produce the platelets on her own, without any supplemental ones that were given, like when when the count dropped below 20. We would be starting the next round of Chemo the following Tuesday, unless for some reason she stopped producing platelets at the current rate. (Last Friday the count was 32). I would not say we turned the corner, but it was a step at the intersection. Next step is to get her to her school's Halloween party on Friday, and Trick or Treating on Sunday.

Angie came and removed Shelly's access so that she could have a bath. Angie had made Shelly sign a contract stating she would not threaten her with bodily harm when she reattached her port, and reaccessed her pain pump. (Angie, as experienced as she was, was not Shelly's hospital nurse, Lucilla, who knew just how to do it). Shelly was still having pain problems, and it hurt us with trying to deal with it.

We went to Shelly's school for the Halloween parade and party on Friday. We were treated by the whole office staff disguised as Waldo, of "Where's Waldo?" fame. Shelly was hurting, but she did visit her class and second grade teacher, Mrs. Luther, and got to visit her first grade teacher, Mrs. Rochford, who had a special bond with Shelly. Because of the noise level and the pain, we left before the parade, but Shelly tried the best she could. She, and Ajay, both went as devils, with red horns. Shelly's outfit was accented with a pitchfork (I sound like a fashion expert). I wore only blue bunny ears on my Indians baseball cap (and the rest of my regular clothes). While talking to the principals, and other parents, one father came up to me, laughing, and called me "the ugliest Playboy bunny he's ever seen".

I responded, in my best Elvis voice "Thank you, Thank you very much", which sounded more like a cross between Elvis and Elmer Fudd. I mean really, how can he mistake the Easter bunny for a Playboy bunny?

After a horrendous Trick or Treat, with only 9 kids begging, and none from our neighborhood, Shelly returned with candy just from our little street. We settled down to watch one of our two favorite shows, "Amazing Race" (SpongeBob being the other one, if you were wondering). During the show a weather report flashed on the screen warning of high winds, as they probably did over half of the U.S. Shelly asked what it said, because like most second graders, she couldn't read that fast. We answered, and she commented "Shouldn't we move our table on the deck?" remembering that a few years ago a limb came down and smashed the glass top. I hadn't thought about it at all, but I know that if Nana had been here that is exactly what she would have said. This little girl brought a tear to my eyes, and joy to my heart. I went out, of course during a commercial, and moved the table. I knew that Shelly was definitely not ready to give up the fight, even as she struggled with her pain.

We went locally and got counts, and her platelet count was up to 95, qualifying her for the second round of Chemo to start the next day. I knew it would be rough on her, and to compound her problems, she had started losing her hair. This kid just didn't get any breaks.

We visited her gymnastics coach (Amy), a wonderful young lady that Shelly loved. Then we went shopping, buying her a new winter jacket. When we got home, her pain returned (if it had ever been gone), and we couldn't get it under control. On top of that, she showed blood around her anus, so, on the advise of the visiting nurse, off we went to the ER again, to be fast tracked into Rainbow Two, the Oncology ward. Ajay stayed with her that night, and they eventually got a room around 11. Shelly's pain was such that they didn't get to sleep until after 2 AM. The next day her platelet count was 11, so she has a transfusion, and the blood around her anus came from something similar to a fissure. Shelly slept most of the day, then after strongly impressing upon the doctors that we wanted to go home, that the low grade fever could be taken care of at home, they finally relented. As the nurse brought the release papers in, Shelly coughed, which was something else that had just started that morning, so the nurse took Shelly's temperature. It was no longer a low grade temperature. It was 102.8 F. We forget about going home, she was staying another night at least. She then proceeded to throw-up, and then had diarrhea to boot. She was definitely staying. She wanted Mommy to stay with her again, and as I kissed my sleepy, sick girl goodbye, with a tear in my eye, she kissed me, and then turned my head, a game we played, and blew bubbles on my cheek. "Oh, no! Not the raspberries" I said.

I went home, had another restless night of sleep, and thought that we would have to scrub going to her school's father-daughter dance on Saturday night. We would be lucky to be home. How my heart ached for her. If only we could get her well, which, considering the cancer, was probably an impossibility. God, how I loved that child. Believe it or not, we got released for the hospital at 4 PM on the day of the dance, with the dance starting at 6. The dance was a gala affair for the girls from the school, all through the third grade. They had food, drink, wild and loud music, and strobe lights. All in all, it was too much for Shelly. When we thought about leaving, we found Shelly's BFF, Josey, and her grandfather Steve, and hooked up with them in a quiet area away from all the activity. We had pictures taken, and then Shelly had to go to the bathroom, and was accompanied by Josey. Next thing I knew, Josey came out and said Shelly needed me, as she had diarrhea. Being in an elementary school and going into a girls restroom didn't seem like the best idea to me, but, with Josey and Steve's assistance, I did it.

We went again locally for counts, and hopefully, she would not need platelets, for which we would have to go to the UH clinic. Shelly was feeling pretty good on Sunday night, so I offered to take us all to Parasson's restaurant in Barberton. Ajay wanted to drive to get in some practice in her new car, so off we went. Ajay took her left hand of the wheel and Shelly commented "Mom, keep both hands on the wheel!"

I chuckled, and said, "Somebody's been reading the drivers manual" to Ajay, and Shelly responded with "I don't remember reading any manual".

We went to UH for a CT scan, and to the clinic for counts. Shelly apparently has developed 'hospitalitis', because her mood would change in an instant to a whinny, crying grouch when we got to clinic, in spite of the tenderness the medical team showed her. She even kicked Dr. Cooke, for which she later apologized. Her counts were acceptable, and no change to her pain regiment. Hopefully we would have a Happy Thanksgiving.

Well, Turkey day had come and gone, and we had a nice meal. We were joined by Cousin Rick and Uncle Steve, who showed up 3 hours late. I didn't know what was going on with him, and I didn't have the time nor the energy to find out. We went shopping on Black

Friday and not Thursday at 8 PM, nor Friday at 6 AM but after lunch. Shelly has outgrown most of her fancy dresses, and with the Ed Bear fund raiser coming up on the following Monday, she needed a new outfit. Although Shelly was in a lot of pain, power shopping seems to bring her out of it (she got that from her Nana). She was walking and darting from outfit to outfit, and making comments like "No Papa, we don't mix strips with plaids". Well, she apparently has never dressed an engineer before, but I relented, and let her pick out what she wanted. We came home, and Ajay went out to practice driving with a friend. Shelly wanted to go back to Penney's to buy some slippers that we forgot, so off we went, although it was snowing and blowing, Shelly didn't mind. On our way back to Penney's Shelly asked me for a couple of dollars. "Why" I asked? "To give them to the bell ringer!" This little girl sure had a big heart.

Later, she wanted to go out for frozen custard, so off we went again. Obviously she was having a good day. We made it back in time for WWE Smackdown, but she retired half way through it.

We went the next Monday to Project Ed Bear, where one of her drawings brought $1100 last year, so she was looking forward to it. This time her drawing only brought $150. On the next day she got her MIBG injection for imaging scans on Wednesday and Thursday, and then the following week she would get an MRI. Hopefully the scans would show good results. She's really looked forward to more snow, so she could have a snowball fight with Papa, and go sled riding. This girl just didn't know the meaning of Quit. Thank God.

Dr. Cooke called. Bad news. The recent chemo did not help. There was very little that could be done for treatment at this time. Shelly had hot spots in her shoulder, her back, her jaw, and at her knees. He was going to talk to the radiation oncologist about possible treatment for those areas, but that wouldn't stop the cancer from progressing throughout her bones. Her CT scan showed no cancer metastasizing in any of her organs, but it continued to progress through her bones. He hoped that she (we) would have a Merry Christmas, but he couldn't say how much time beyond that. He talked with the Hospice and Palliative Care team about pain control, but that was about it.

I thanked everybody for their prayers and gifts, but it's looked like it was time for Shelly to go to Jesus, and see Nana and (Great) Grandpa and Grandma. I really didn't know what else to say, our pain would not end when Shelly's did.

We went to the hospital on December 4, and Shelly's count were good, so she didn't need a transfusion of platelets or anything else. Dr. Cooke stated that, because the cancer has not metastasized to any of her organs, and, hopefully the MRI of her head on Thursday would show nothing in the way of a tumor, then the tumors in her bones was NOT life threatening, but there was that 'yet' that was implied, but not stated. We were still trying to deal with her extreme pain as she was changed to a Fentenyl pump, thinking that her body had built up some resistance to the Dilaudid (her current pump). Compounding things was the season, and the number of people that were reaching out to us, not that I was complaining, but controlling Shelly's pain was our only priority.

The following day we went on the Polar Express, and Shelly had a happy day. She had asked to be detached from her pump while on the train, as she was very conscientious about it, and wanted the freedom that other kids had. As the other kids were singing Christmas carols, Shelly needed to get away. Our former neighbor, Polly, who was a volunteer Conductor, took her to the Pullman Car, where she and other Conductors bought Shelly gifts (like she needed more). She also got to see Santa first, and exclusively, in that car. It was very good for Shelly.

I had been concerned, but not greatly so, about my son, Steve, who hadn't been around much, and was usually late or a no-show for activities. Shelly truly loved her uncle, and it hurt me to see him neglect her by not showing up when he said he would. She would even call him when he was late and ask him where he was. Steve had purchased Great Grandpa and Grandma's house, which was right up the street from Cousin Rick. Cousin Rick called and said that there were police cars at Steve's house, a lot of them, and that he would go up to see what was going on, and call us back. He reported on the call back that Steve had been arrested, for using and manufacturing crystal methaphetamine (crystal meth), along with five or six others in his house. Although I felt much anguish, I could not get dragged into Steve's problems, and I kept my focus on Shelly's treatment. Steve was an adult, and as far as I was concerned, it was his problem, not mine. You may call me callus or cold if you like, but it was what it was.

Dr. Cooke called me from the airport before he was to depart to a conference in San Diego, where he was speaking. He said that Shelly's MRI showed no tumors in her brain, and that there was some improvement from the last MRI. He also said that there was a hot spot in the middle of her back, on her spinal cord, and that was probably the basis of her back pain, and some of her instability and lack of strength in her legs. He said he forwarded the images to the Radiation Oncologist to see if he felt that local radiation treatment would help alleviate the pain. He asked us to evaluate the need and discomfort that Shelly would be going through, getting additional radiation treatment. We talked briefly with Shelly, and she still wanted to wait until after Christmas for any further treatment. We would honor her wish.

Many things were happening, and, were happening quickly. On December 7th, a Santa came along with an entourage of elves and friends, and brought gifts for Shelly, and Rigatoni for us. The keyboard that they brought for Shelly didn't work, so off Santa went to Toys-R-Us (boy, talk about a glutton for punishment) to exchange it. After escaping the hoards of kids by running over some with his reindeer, he returned with a working unit. He, and his elf's, and Heather and her husband then watched (you guessed it, it was Friday night after all) WWE Smackdown. Shelly tired by 9 O'clock, and after Santa's entourage left, we went to bed, with Shelly making me promised that I tell her who had won between Shamus and Del Rio.

Shelly was in a good mood, and she seemed pretty (I could end this sentence here) happy. The following morning she went with her mother to buy a replacement for the fish that the aquarium filter ate. Later that Saturday we went to Cleveland Hopkins for United Airlines' Fantasy flight, a busy day, with, hopefully, Shelly getting a nap or two someplace.

On the United Airlines Fantasy Flight they flew us on a 737 to the North Pole in 45 minutes, and then we deplaned to a sit down dinner, with Santa, crafts, and face painting, among others. Unfortunately for us, the noise was too loud on the plane, and Shelly was in a lot of pain. As we were landing, they requested that we pull all the shades down on the windows (where else would the shades be?) so that we wouldn't disturb the reindeer grazing in the field. Shelly left hers up a little bit, and peaked through and exclaimed "They have a Steak and Shake, and a Target store, look! There's a Giant Eagle!" Nothing got by this little girl, and she started to warm up some. At the party Shelly went up to Santa and he asked what she wanted for Christmas. Shelly replied "a Hot Wheels Loop, a Polaroid Camera, and for Santa to take her Cancer away".

I knew Santa had a tear in his eye, as did I. I prayed "Please God, hear my plea, don't take Shelly from us, I know you want her, but isn't there another way to get rid of her pain? Please Jesus, help!" It hurt me so when she's in pain, and there was nothing we could do.

I had received a couple of e-mail Christmas cards. Being old fashioned I would rather have received an actual card, but, these people thought enough of me to send a card, so I didn't complain. One card had an interesting verse in it: "...It takes a minute to find a special person, an hour to appreciate them, a day to love them, and an entire life to forget them".

I had been fortunate to have two such people be an integral part of my life. My wife, Bonnie, who, when I meet old friends, they talk about what they remember about her, how she took stands, and earned everybody's respect. They usually have very little to say about what I did, or didn't do, and that was OK, because for the most part I wasn't an activist, and I didn't make waves. I had 47 years with Bonnie, but that wasn't enough, I would have liked 47 more, or until I died.

The other person, of course was Shelly. This vibrant little girl still warmed the shackles of my heart. People that knew her, know that she is special. But, I think all parents feel that way about their children. My heart went out to the parents of Newtown, on the tragedy that happened there, where one father spoke in similar terms about his precious six year old daughter. Such a waste. I had Shelly for 8-1/2 years, and I would like another 8-1/2 years, or 47, but I feared that it was not going to happen. I didn't look pass that, not knowing how I was going to go on. I was reminded of Ray Charles lyrics "...but time has stood still since we've been apart".

Shelly had been doing somewhat better, with Kerri and Ann from Camp Quality coming over and playing Headband, cards, and (Disney's) Scene-it, making all of us laugh frequently. She was looking forward to Tuesday when we were going to the WWE Smackdown in Pittsburgh. I wondered if Gorgeous George and Don Eagle were on the card?

The elves that came Friday had two extra tickets for WWE Smackdown (in Pittsburgh), and asked Shelly and I to join Brendon and John Danes (another bucket list item). Shelly had a minor breakdown because she didn't have a (well) coordinated outfit (yea, go figure), so a last minute trip to Wally World fixed that. We drove to the Danes house near Lake Milton, and went from there to Pittsburgh with them. When we got there, Shelly warmed up, and got in the mood to shop, where she went through the gift shop and spent a lot of John's money (he wouldn't let me pay). We had great seats, but we had to climb down a lot of steps, which took a toll on Shell. After watching a number of matches, and eating hot dogs and nachos and cheese, Shelly got tired and we left early, but not before we stopped to shop some more, this time (fortunately) on my dime. Honestly, I think she would rather be turned loose in a mall with a credit card (is it a female thing?) then endure the loud noises of WWE. All in all, it was a very enjoyable evening. Shelly settled down on the way home, and talked John's ear off. We went to the hospital the following day bearing gifts, hoping that they had good news about a breakthrough, or something, anything, that will help.

Christmas came, and apparently someone had spread the rumor that Shelly was a deprived child, that she didn't have much. Nothing was farther from the truth. Shelly has visited Santa on the Polar Express, on her Fantasy flight, and, even the staff at UH Hospitals bought into it. Santa even came to visit courtesy of Heather, Shane, and the Danes family. The Hospital took the cake. Their Santa gave her 5 presents, then the Oncology staff another three. Oh yeah, the Steven J. Cannale Cancer Foundation gave her a digital camera.

With all these gifts already under the tree, people were still asking what she wanted. I mean, give me a break. I DIDN'T KNOW! I know, I shouldn't be yelling, but I was as frustrated as everybody else. Everything she saw on a commercial she said she wanted, but by the time the next commercial came on, that changed (it's that FEMALE thing again).

Her counts were good four days before Christmas, and we didn't have go back to the clinic for 2 to 3 weeks. I thought about getting another tree to accommodate the overflow, but it was too late. I couldn't even get my dining room table cleaned to have my family over.

Well, the Jolly, old, fatman visited on Christmas Eve. (No, It wasn't me). Shelly and I visited the Whitlam's, our neighbors, on Christmas Eve, (they did invite us, and Shelly wore her reindeer antlers) and enjoyed a fine meal. Once again Shelly received way too many gifts. We came home because she wanted to make chocolate milk to go with the cookies Ajay made (remembering Santa didn't like chocolate chip). After setting up for the fatman (me, in this case), and, sorry, Rudolph, no carrots, we retired. Although Shelly had insisted that her bed be cleared off for her to sleep in her own bed, she slept with me, as usual.

We had a small gathering of family for our traditional dinner, with Cousin Rick and Steve joining us, with Steve arriving late, it appeared he was still doing drugs, but I didn't take issue with him, especially on Christmas. It was a relatively peaceful day, with Shelly getting two naps.

A call from Dr. Cooke on Christmas day, plus a call from good friend Shirley had brightened our holiday.

The only 'downer' was when my brother called the day after (Christmas) and told me he took our mother to the hospital, because she had severe pain in her right leg. I planned on visiting her before a major storm was supposed to hit.

We were still looking into additional radiation possibly in January to combat Shelly's back pain. Pain was still a big issue, and it hurt to see Shelly in extreme pain. We got through Christmas, and Shelly had some relatively good days. She was still struggling with pain, so the nurse increased her pain pump medication. The Friday after Christmas was a perfect day to go out in the snow. Shelly wanted to shovel and have a snowball fight with Papa, but it ended up with Papa shoveling and Shelly having a snowball fight. Afterward, we followed deer tracks through our yard, and then did some sledding down the side yard, propelled by Papa. That exhausted her, but it brought a smile (and a tear) to Papa, knowing that she wanted to go out and did so.

We went out to eat that evening, and had to stop and shop at Cracker Barrel after eating at Parasson's. Yea, go figure, like she needed to shop (it was that female thing again). New Year's came, and went. Shelly and I tried to stay up (well, we were watching TV from bed) to watch the Ball drop. Needless to say, Shelly was asleep, and I followed shortly thereafter. We had our traditional Pork and Sauerkraut on the First, with Steve being late again. I still can't get involved with him.

When I wore a younger man's clothes (to quote Billy Joel), actually some people say I'm still wearing the same clothes, but I digressed, I used to think that old people probably just sat on the porch and watched the grass grow, thinking about, when is nap time? In the years since I retired, my twilight years, but I didn't think about much, nor did I watch the grass grow (It was hard under 6 inches of snow). But my mind set seemed like it really hadn't changed much since I was 25. Sure, I had done a lot of things that were really stupid at that time, and I felt lucky that I didn't get in trouble, but things were different then, which really wasn't a good excuse. I felt that, at my age, I've matured, but I'm still, to an extent, that 'happy go lucky' guy that I was at twenty five. But my maturity, if that's what it was, caused me to think before I spoke, which was good, and was a good rule for anyone.

Some people had said, "Jim, you've given Shelly 4 extra years, you've done all that you can do". Well, I still didn't feel that. I wanted to give her more, but I didn't know what or how to accomplish that, and knew for sure that it wasn't in my power. I was there for her when she needed me, or needed anything, but that was not enough for me. I wanted 4 or 40 more years, but it wasn't in the cards. I prayed

"God, I know you want her, but there's so much I want to do with her. Hear my plea, my prayer, and perform a miracle on Shelly, and let her live. Let her beat this terrible disease, in Jesus name, Amen."

Shelly had a really good day Monday, January 7th. We went to our favorite Barberton chicken house, and on the way back, she asked me if she would have to repeat second grade. I told her that, if she didn't go to school anymore this year, that she would have to. She told me that she missed Mrs. Rochford, Mrs. McLean, Mrs. Luther, the principals, and Mrs. Brutz, the Librarian. I suggested that we could go for a visit when she was up to it. When we got home, she wanted to play cards, so Shelly, Ajay and I played. I start grumbling and talking gibberish about the girls ganging up on me, and got Shelly laughing, which got all of us laughing. She then commented "this must be a Country Club, and we're all drunk", which really got us laughing. It was so good to hear her laugh and be happy, because she hadn't laughed hardly at all for the last three months. It was definitely a moment to cherish.

The next day we went to the hospital and talked to the radiation oncologist, Dr. Mansur, who said some radiation on one spot on her back would help her pain. The schedule got set up for a CT scan on the next Friday, followed by ten spot radiation treatments on that location. This is only to get her pain under better control, and is not a treatment leading to a cure. We need God's healing hand for a cure.

At the end of Shelly's radiation treatment it would be 5 years since we've been living this nightmare. Four and a half years ago Akron Children's told us that there was no more that they could do. That we had better go home and prepare. St. Jude's told us not to come there, that they could not help us. Cleveland Clinic said what a precious, active, fun little girl, but they couldn't help us. Well, now, there's no more treatment, only pain control, and this series of radiation treatments is the last treatment Shelly would get. From here on out, they would deal with pain control by medication.

Those of you that knew Shelly early on marveled at what a happy, fun little girl she was. Now, she was bitter. She was hurting big time. She didn't do much. Excitement for her was watching a new video with Mommy and Papa, although she often fell asleep during them. Gone are the days when she would give us some wisdom, and wit. Although the other day, during a video nap, she woke up and asked "How do squirrels know where they hide their nuts?" I stammered for an answer, and she rolled over and went back to sleep before I could answer. It seemed like it took her forever to get her weight up to 40 lbs., and now she's pushing 70 lbs. Inactivity and steroids do that.

Shelly had been poked, cut, stabbed, flipped and had been subjected to so many other procedures at many hospitals, all in the name of helping her, of comforting her, of maybe finding a cure, but to no avail. She now cries, and insults the staff, often trying to kick them, but never pleasant towards the medical people who truly cared for her. I was told she had earned the right to be angry, to cry, to lash out, but it was still hard for me to deal with. I guess if I had everything done to me that she had, then I would probably do the same.

As we neared the end, I look back over the five years, and it's hard not to feel sad about everything that had happened to us. We lost Great Grandpa Woods almost six years ago, then Great Grandma Woods 4 years ago (he was 98, she 101), and then my wife of 47 years, Bonnie (Nana) in October, 2011. I had not envisioned this being the road that I would walk down. I knew that Jesus walked with me, but the burden wasn't any lighter. I didn't want to look beyond, because I could see nothing. My vision of Easy Street had been smashed long ago. My mother is almost 94, and was in a rehab facility, and she's starting to lose her faculties. I had envisioned that Bonnie and I would be taking cruises with Shelly, but that will not happen. I can't even take Shelly to Disney, not that we don't want to go, but with the amount of sleep she needs daily to fight the pain, we would be sleeping in a motel in Orlando, with our support people back in Ohio.

It' had been a long road, and we have run out of options. We needed Divine intervention.

Believe it or not, with the weather cooperating (sort of), and with Shelly willing, we made a trip to the Cleveland Zoo. When we got there, around 10, it was still cold, so we went into the rain forest.

Once inside, Shelly wanted to walk, which really surprised me, but that was OK, as she would soon tire anyway, and I would push her in her wheelchair. But she surprised me, and walked throughout the rain forest. When we were done there, of course after visiting the gift shop, I wheeled her into the zoo. She rode (in her wheelchair) to see the elephants, and then she wanted to see the primates and the big cats, so we took the shuttle to the upper area of the Primate building location.

Once again she surprised me, walking throughout the building, and, after boarding the tram again, we went to the northern territory, and debarked. She walked again, saw the polar bear and the penguins, rode a little, and then walked to see the wolves, where we once again boarded the tram to take us back to the main gate, where, surprise, surprise, we visited another gift shop (she was never too sore to shop).

All in all, we had a great day. I know it wasn't much for a normal child, but I had to enjoy what little happiness she gave me. It appeared that the radiation was helping with the pain, as evident by that day's outing, but it was still too early to tell, and we wouldn't know for how long it would work.

I knew Shelly was wondering, about death. I knew this conversation was coming.

"Papa, am I going to die from my Cancer?"

"Yes, Shelly, you are. We all are going to die."

"Is there any more treatments for my cancer?"

"No, Shell, at this time there is nothing else that the doctors are aware of"

"My radiation treatments, they're just for pain?"

"Yes, only for pain"

"Will the cancer spread to other parts of my body?"

"According to the doctors, yes"

"Then will I die?"

"Unless there is a new treatment, yes. But God only knows when, and he may take somebody old, like me instead"

"No! I don't want him to take you, or Mommy"

"Shell, God determines who to take, and when"

"I'll be right back"

Shell disappeared for 5 minutes, then reappeared, and asked "Will I go into third grade?"

"Shelly, if you want to go into third grade with your classmates, then you have to go back to school. Or, you will have to repeat second grade next year, and then go into third grade"

"If I go to school, will I be able to have recess?"

"Shelly, we can work out the details when you go. Maybe you could go into the Library, or to the Principals office, and do something with them"

She pondered this, then took her nighttime medicine, and said "Let's go up to bed"

As we were climbing the stairs, she said that she made Mommy cry. "How come?" I asked.

"I asked her the same thing I asked you, and we cried together"

After I tucked her in bed, I told her not to give up hope, because God may work one of his miracles. I kissed and hugged her goodnight, extra tight, because I didn't want her to see the tears in my eyes. I wondered when I would have this conversation with her, and how it would come about. Now I knew.

I was ready to throw in the towel. I couldn't bear watching the pain Shelly was going through. I mean, how bad was it for her if I couldn't bear it? I prayed for God to end her pain. If this was how the rest of her life was going to be, then please take her now.

The next day it took an hour to get her out of bed to take her for her next to last radiation treatment. She was in such excruciating pain that she cried all the way to the UH Hospital in Cleveland. Her Dilaudid pain pump just wasn't getting it. A phone call to the clinic had them pave the way to get her admitted, to get the pain under control. After trying to get the pain pump adjusted high enough for a higher level of Dilaudid, which couldn't be done, the pain doctor decided to put her on Methadone, starting at a low level. This adjustment has improved her pain immensely, and we were released home, where she was sleeping comfortably on the couch watching (don't ask me how she watches in her sleep) 'SHREK'.

Shelly was continuing to fight. We went out to eat, and Shelly, still a little (?) doped up, asked for whipped cream on her spaghetti.

Then on the way home, she wanted to stop for custard at Strickland's, and went in with me. After being served, I realized I left my money in the car, so I said I would be right back. After returning and paying for her custard, she said they asked her if she had been ice skating. She replied, "No, I have cancer" Boy, talk about a show stopper.

In the first week of February, Shelly asked when she was going to get sedated. We replied that she wasn't going to, that that would have been for the first Radiation treatment when they had to make a form for your face. I replied "There's no more sedation because there is no more treatment."

Shelly, confused, said "No more Chemo?"

"No Shell, nothing. You said you wanted no more treatments, so that is what is going to happen. If you want more, we will talk to Dr. Cooke next Tuesday, but there is very little left that can be done."

"You mean that I'm just going to die?" she replied.

I know she was hoping for a different answer, but I said "Yes Shell, we've had this discussion before, we all are going to die sometime. The Radiation treatments were to ease the pain. Just like the Methadone pain pump that you are now using. For pain control only. It's OK for you to leave, to see Jesus and Nana."

"Grandpa said before he died (Great Grandpa Woods, passed in 2007, before Shelly was diagnosed) that when he got to Heaven that he was going to build a big house, with rooms for all of us. My room was going to be decorated in hearts. Mommy, what's your room going to decorated like?" Ajay was sort of taken aback by her question. She asked me on the side, how do you answer a question like that.

"From the heart" I replied.

Shelly then said "Papa's room was going to have squirrels" I didn't know where that came from, but I didn't rebut it.

Every night when I tucked Shelly in bed, I would kiss her and tell her I love her, and comment "we'll have a better day tomorrow". She usually nods, or says OK, or just smiles. Today she replied "I doubt it". That hurt my heart more that the lack of treatment discussion. She's sleeping more and more, but doesn't appear to be in much pain. I just wanted a lot more time with her. Please God, grant my wish.

My little girl, I was so proud of her; she was a fighter. She didn't just want to go peacefully into the night. Shelly wanted to go shopping at Cracker Barrel (big surprise) for a robe with a hood on it. I suggested that we go to Target, because Cracker Barrel doesn't carry that kind of thing. She agreed, so off we went to Target, where she rode in a (shopping) cart through the store hunting for a robe with a hood. No luck. Shelly suggested we try WallyWorld (Wall Mart for the uninformed), so off we went again. When we parked the car, Shell said that she wanted to walk. OK, her mother and I exchanged glances, like, sure, but we let her. Well, to show us, she walked all the way to the children's department at the rear of the store, and then, not finding a robe, picked up three St. Patrick's Day shirts. She then proceeded to walk all the way out (not with the shirts, I paid for them).

We went to the clinic on Tuesday, February 12, and nobody knew we were coming except Dr. Cooke. We still got in, quite quickly, and saw Dr. Cooke and the pain management team. Shelly had wanted to ask Dr. Cooke about more treatments, so I asked (for her), as Shelly was a little drowsy. He said that there is another medicine that will possibly slow Neuroblastoma, but not defeat it, but it has some side effects, and her counts must be good. We agreed to try it, be a pill (which Shelly woke up enough to insist on), providing her counts stayed good. We also would have her put on a stimulant, like Ritalin, although maybe not that specific drug, to help give her more awake time. We came home, and she insisted I take her to Video Game Exchange, then to Strictland's again for frozen custard. She always tries the flavor of the day, today being Key Lime, but always settles for Vanilla. Because she's a regular there (4 times a week), or maybe because she's so precious, her custard was comped, as was one of her videos (they really loved her at the Video Game Exchange).

I felt the end was near. Shelly couldn't walk. She wanted to go to the Olive Garden, but once we got her dressed, she couldn't move her legs, so we ordered pickup. At bedtime we had to carry her up the steps, and that morning she had to be carried down. We had the nurse come, and she increased her pain medication. She also ordered a hospital bed for us, so we would have to rearrange our living room to accommodate it.

I wanted to say I felt her pain, I shared her pain, but I couldn't. I didn't know what pain she had, but it can't be shared with anybody but Jesus. I had my own pain to deal with. Her mother had her own pain. We loved her so much, but, we wanted her out of pain. Maybe it was selfish of me, of us, but, I prayed "Jesus please take her pain. Please take her into Your loving arms and let her romp through the clover, let her laugh with Nana, let her sit on (great) Grandpa's lap and eat strawberries prepared by him. Let her enjoy her room that Grandpa said he was going to make for her. Let her make You smile. Please answer my prayer, dear Jesus."

On February 20, 2013, I posted on CaringBridge:

Family and Friends:

I don't have the strength or the phone numbers to call all of you that care for Shelly. Shelly is no longer in pain. She passed this morning in her sleep after the pain became under control, but not enough strength to fight the horrible disease that has ravaged her body. Please continue to pray for all the other children that are fighting this terrible disease as Shelly earned her Angel wings after 5 years of fighting.

Thank you and God Bless,
Jim

with Rev. Carol

with Rob Christopher - Hugs N Bugs

with Uncle Steve

Ten

DOES LIFE GO ON?

THE SERVICE

The night before Shelly passed, the visiting nurse was here, Angie, Ajay and her boyfriend Fabio, and myself. It was around 8 o'clock, and Dr. Cooke called and said he wanted to come and see Shelly tonight. He must have had a premonition, because he didn't want to wait until the morning as I had suggested. It was quiet, and Shelly was resting, but not quite asleep when he arrived. He spoke to her and kissed her, and she was pleased to see him. As he left, he said a few kind words to me, and we cried together. It was heart-wrenching. Shelly fell asleep, and an overnight nurse arrived, so that Ajay and I could get some sleep. Ajay had last contact with her when she helped Shell go to the bathroom around 4 AM. In the morning I came down and went to Shell, and she was cold. She had passed in her sleep. She was no longer in pain. I called my brother and Susie, and they both said they were coming over. I could not reach Shirley, but she showed up unknowing that Shelly had passed in the night. Angie had come and officially pronounced her dead. I called the funeral home, and they came around 2 PM to take Shelly. We had a house full of people, and Shelly was laying there, dead. Shelly's cat, Smokey, who never left her side, was still there at her side. I personally lifted Shelly and placed her on the gurney to be taken, after which I completely broke down. Everybody else in the house was also crying. It seemed so final, yet we all knew it was coming. How do you prepare for it? If this was a test of my faith, then I was failing it. I hurt so much, but I had to go on. I was angry at God, but I had asked him to stop Shelly's pain, and He did.

Arrangements had to be made. I had previously contacted Billows' Funeral Home, the one that was storing our casket that we purchased over 4 years ago. We had to go and finalize the arrangements. We had to notify the church, write the obituary, arrange the meal, get somebody the run the service. So many things.

We had not been going to church. Bonnie and I were Baptists, and went to a Methodist church when we lived in Madison. Bonnie's folks were life long members of the Akron Baptist Temple, and Bonnie and I were still on their membership roll. I didn't want someone impersonal to perform Shelly's service. I wanted someone who knew her, who could speak from the heart about her. I wanted Rev. Carol, but she had moved. I asked Chaplain Mike, of Rainbow Babies to perform the service, and he gladly accepted. I felt that I should inform Rev. Carol, because she may not get word of Shelly's passing living in Indiana. I called her, and she said, "Oh Jim, I'm coming! Send me the details."

I asked her if she would be willing to perform the service with Chaplain Mike, and she said "Of course!" So that detail was taken care of. With the assistance of the staff at Billows, the rest of the details fell into place. We would have calling hours twice on Sunday at Billows, and the funeral service would be at the main sanctuary of the Akron Baptist Temple at One o'clock.

In addition to the obituary being in the Beacon Journal, a beautiful article was written by Jewell Cardwell, complete with pictures of Shelly, a true testament to the fight Shelly put up.

From Seattle my daughter Elaine and granddaughter Megan came. My other granddaughter, Sarah came from Chicago. So many people came during calling hours, although Steve spent just a nominal amount of time at the funeral home. I guess we all mourn in our own way. Family, friends, relatives, strangers came. Jewell Cardwell came, and it was a surprise to me, although it shouldn't have been. Even Jewell cried. Of all the people that gave their respects, and sentiments, I probably remember Jewell's the most. She said to me "Jim, you had done everything humanly possible for Shelly. You made a 'road map' that others could follow."

Members of the hospital staff came, Shelly's school principals, teachers, classmates. The Hospice staff showed up. Even her preschool teacher, from five years earlier came. I was overwhelmed.

Just when I thought I had my emotions under control, someone would mention something that Shelly had done, and the tears would start again. Christopher Milo came with his kids, and he broke down. Shelly was very special to him. The staff from Camp Quality, Shelly's companions, Karla and Kelly came.

For the One o'clock funeral service I told Ajay that I intended to be there at noon, and that she should be there no later than 12:30. I asked her if she knew how to get there, after all, she had gone to Sunday School there when she was young, and we had the meal after Bonnie's funeral there. She assured me that she did, after all, she had her Garman (GPS).

By 12:30, people had started arriving, but no Steve, no Ajay. I started greeting people, and many asked where Ajay was. I suppressed my anger. Cousin Rick came to me and said that Ajay had called him for directions. I was starting to fume. Even Steve wasn't there. What was going on? Ten minutes later Rick informed me that Ajay had called again, still lost. She arrived at 12:55, and greeted the later arrivals. But people that had arrived earlier got up to pay their respects to her. Steve had arrived somewhere between.

The service started with Chaplain Mike and Rev. Carol officiating. Rev. Carol told of the early years of Shelly's treatments, and her interacting with Shell.

Eulogy-Homily for Shelly
Carol (Harrison) Barrett
25 February 2013

When I grow up, I want to be just like Shelly: rock star queen, alligator hunter, a comedian, spiritual princess. She was the most amazing child we have ever met. For me, she was the most alive human being I have ever known. I met Shelly while I served as staff chaplain at Akron Children's Hospital. When she was just 3 going on 30, I was paged to accompany Shelly and Ajay to radiology, where our heroine wove a thread of humor into her X-ray experience as she did everything else at one point crying out, "Mommy! Papa! Smokey! Somebody, save me!"

That dramatic humor kept her and everyone else laughing amidst the pain and tears. One afternoon I came to call. It was nap time. Nana, Bonnie, insisted it was OK for all of us there to talk. Then suddenly, from beneath the hospital bed covers bubbled out, "Pipe down over there! Can't you see someone is trying to sleep?!" Jim in perfect Rodney Dangerfield fashion chuckled back, "You're killing me kid! You're killing me!" We laughed and laughed, and yet, it still hurt.

Hospital rounds as many of you may know can be at best confusing for families. For patients, especially children, it can be terrifying. There is the rounding oncologist, the head nurse on duty, the pharmacologist, the psychologist, child life specialist, social worker, nutritionist, chaplain, and if you are a teaching hospital, several residents., all moving from patient to patient, from one room to the next, almost like a group of tourists at the local zoo.

It's not unusual for pediatric patients to hide under their sheets, waiting for the tourists to go away. Not Shelly. Each day, during rounds, she'd get on all fours, on the floor or on her bed, and pace quietly to and fro as team members asked and answered questions and delivered reports. Ignored too long, the little feline Shelly would give a little swat, let out a soft growl. "What are you today," someone would eventually ask. "A lion or a tiger?" She'd wait until we would throw her some imaginary wildcat breakfast.

She was something. She knew how to transform the ordinary of routine into extraordinary. She took the "scary" and turned it into fun for everyone. Just recalling these scenarios makes us all beam with smiles. Still, it hurts.

A child with cancer was asked how she learned to be so brave. She learned by watching Shelly. "My friend Shelly is 'bery' brave." It warms our hearts to be reminded of just how much purpose this little girl had. And still, it hurts. I remember Bonnie telling of the day when they were driving away from the hospital when Shelly suddenly yelled out, "Dr. Trash! Dr. Trash!" She saw him through the van window as he was walking on the sidewalk. He had gone in and out of her room to care for her just as the physicians had done. So, of course, he was Dr. Trash.

Some time a long time later after Shelly required a different treatment from another facility, Bonnie called to have me track down Dr. Trash. Shelly needed to make sure he was still praying for her. Bonnie wanted him to know how Shelly was doing and how valued he was. It is so amazing to see how God's love poured out through Shelly and her family long after she had left the hospital. And still, it hurts.

One day Bonnie was quite discouraged but when I visited that night, Shelly was exuberant. "Rev. Carol! Rev. Carol! Guess who called me on the phone today? And look at the autographed picture he sent to my room!" Bonnie said Kermit the Frog had phoned the room and asked to speak with Shelly. She didn't know what he told Shelly but the little Muggin Head held onto that with all her might. Everyone here today and many others as well, did more than impersonating a muppet to help this little girl beat the odds. You did whatever you could, whenever you could, however large or small. And still, it hurts.

While other children were singing veggie tales and sesame street songs, Shelly had her favorite: a song by Tom Petty, "I Won't Back Down". She didn't understand all the lyrics (she would sing "gates of pale" instead of "gates of hell", for example), but her soul and spirit totally "got" the song. When she sang it, her little body turned her into a force not to be reckoned with! To this day, I receive great strength from God through seeing Shelly sitting on her bed, headphones on and CD playing, singing:

"You can stand me up at the gates of hell, but I won't back down...
With fisted hands, arms swinging away:
...I got just one life. In a world that keeps on pushing me around,
I'll stand my ground and I won't back down."

And the stories go on and on and on. And so must we. So how will we? How can we? The question for us I believe is this: will we let God's little shepherdess lead us to the Master? Can we continue to huddle together, around the shepherd's crook she left behind (whatever that might look like for each of us), and lean into the Master, the Holy Spirit Jesus promised to send so that we would not be orphaned?

For me that hook comes in the form of a poem I have rewritten, called "To Honor You" It was edited by my former colleague, Karen Ballard before I adapted it for Shelly.

To Honor You
Adapted by Rev. Carol Barrett

To honor you, I will get up every morning and take a deep breath
And start another day without you in it.
Rev. Carol modified the poem, continuing,
To Honor You honor you, I will ask everyone I know to EAT A JELLY FOR SHELLY and post the photo on my Facebook page.
To honor you, I will sing "I Won't Back Down"
   at the top of my lungs with the windows rolled down.
Now I will live for us both so that all I do,
I do to honor you.   Amen.

Chaplain Mike talked about the last year of her treatment, how a person's life is reflected by the 'dash' on their tombstone, the one between the date of their birth and the date they left this earth. How Shelly's life was much more than a dash, how she had touched so many people in her short life, how she showed how to keep fighting. He then opened it up to the audience, if any of them wanted to say anything.

Dr. Cooke got up and gave a true testimony about the fight that this little girl had in her. He was close to breaking up, as his words brought many to tears.

In Loving Memory of Shelly Thornton (July 28th 2004 to Feb 20th 2013)

Good afternoon. My name is Dr. Ken. It is truly an honor and a privilege for me to say a few words about our beloved Shelly. In doing so, I hope to share with you the impact this little girl had on so many of us at Rainbow.

Shelly began her battle against Neuroblastoma over 5 years ago. As many of you know, doctors first believed that she had arthritis in her hip. However, after many tests and several weeks of antibiotics, her intense pain persisted and it was finally determined that Shelly had stage IV Neuroblastoma. Unremitting pain would be the ominous signature of this terrible disease and the "thorn" that would plague Shelly over the course of time. As it turns out, Neuroblastoma is the 2nd most common solid tumor affecting kids Shelly's age, and as the "stage IV" might suggest, this tumor had already spread throughout her body. Powerful chemotherapy drugs were soon started, but the tumor didn't budge. After several months of therapy, the medical team told the family there was nothing more that they could do.

Well, I wasn't in the room for that conversation, and I am sure most of you here today knew Bonnie Thornton – "Nana" – so let's just say that this was NOT going to go over very well!! No sir...Not at all!! Letting nothing stand in their way of getting Shelly's cancer under control, the family contacted doctors at the Children's Hospital of Philadelphia where Shelly received two rounds of experimental, cutting edge therapy that for the first time... would bring Shelly's NBL to its knees...but now what? What were the next steps?

In was at this point in the Summer of 2009 that with defenses down and the trust of a child, Bonnie, Jim, Ajay and Shelly turned to my team at Rainbow for more answers, more help and importantly for continued hope that they would win this battle. While Neuroblastoma is treatable, Shelly's tumor already showed its teeth by not responding to conventional therapy so we knew that chemotherapy alone would not be sufficient....Shelly would need a blood stem cell transplant. Hence, with our sights still set on cure, and with a combination of calm, determination and confidence that soon became the family's trademark, Shelly embarked on an aggressive regimen that included high dose chemo followed first by an infusion of her own stem cells and ultimately by radiation. As hoped, the treatment was associated with early success and I can still remember sharing with Jim, Bonnie and Ajay the news that Shelly was now in complete remission – a state where cancer can no longer been detected. "Cure" however is remission over time and unfortunately, true to form, Shelly's tumor would return aggressive as ever, less than 18 months following her transplant. I remember a point in December of 2010...Shelly wasn't feeling well, she was sleepy and had thrown up a few times. I directed Jim and Bonnie to the local ER where Shelly faded into near unresponsiveness. She was life flighted to Rainbow and a CT scan revealed a mass in the brain. Emergency surgery showed mainly blood – a hemorrhage if you will - but close examination of the hemorrhage sac revealed a few tiny, round, blue, cells indicative of NBL...Shelly's tumor had returned

During this dark and challenging time, two things shined through with an unquenchable radiance: 1. Shelly's incredible will to live and 2. Bonnie and Jim's unblemished devotion and commitment to each other and their beloved grand-daughter. Always at Shelly's side the family never lost hope that she would recover, and they confidently and courageously made critical decisions that gave her every chance to be here with us today.

- the recurrence of this terrible disease, not once, not twice but three times,
- the return of relentless pain and
- ultimately in the untimely death of our beloved daughter, grand daughter, patient and friend.

It is in the midst of the intense sadness that fills our hearts today that it is so very important to realize that this fight represented much more than simply the loss of a wonderful little girl, for what unfolded during this five year period can only be described as a remarkable struggle for life through which shined...

- The ever-present love and support of an incredible group of friends and family
- The inner strength and courage of a wonderful little girl who reached out and touched us all
- And the incredible, sacrifice of a devoted grandmother, grandfather and mother to the "love of their life".

I was one of many physicians who had the privilege of caring for Shelly. Dr. Egler, my assistant and "right hand" Linda, Shelly's nurse Lucilla and I had the honor of being dubbed "Shelly's Angels" a designation and responsibility all of us embraced and accepted with both pride and humility

During this time I developed the utmost respect and admiration for Bonnie, Jim and Ajay. Throughout our relatively brief relationship, I have come to recognize that they are truly great people whose genuine kindness was superseded only by their love and devotion to one another. Despite their vulnerable position, they were a pleasure to work with; always pleasant, never on time for Shelly's appointments.... and forever grateful to the doctors, nurses and staff in whom they entrusted Shelly's care.

I also was able to appreciate the way the family functioned as an inseparable team...rarely were they not all together:

Shelly: the spunky, "invincible" patient with a fiery personality and incredible spirit.

Bonnie the proud, resilient, outspoken, - did I tell you that Bonnie would let you know what was on her mind!?? - loving grandmother who was always there to help absorb the bad news and to make all of the tough decisions

Jim who's charming and calming personality provided comfort to Shelly in times of crisis and formed the foundation from which the family drew their energy and strength. And...

Ajay: the ultimate protector and advocate for her beloved daughter, insuring that we always kept Shelly's feelings, comfort and dignity in mind when making treatment decisions.

This partnership, along with the support of their wonderful sphere friends, many of you are here with us today, allowed the Thorntons' to take control of, rather than be controlled by, even the most frightening situations and to approach challenges with confidence, clarity of thought, and determination.

In his hit song "Future, Love Paradise" the singer – song writer Seal begins:

But if only you could see them, you would know from their faces
They were Kings and queens followed by princes and princesses
They were future power people, sharing love with the loveless
Shinning the light, because they wanted it seen.....

My dear friends, there is no question in my mind that Shelly was a princess on this earth...During the last several years, I savored every opportunity to get a glimpse of the true princess Shelly was...a vibrant, funny loving, girl with the charisma to light up a room with her huge smile. Just like all of you, we at Rainbow were attracted to Shelly; when she was well, her magnetism and charm were so very palpable....as Bonnie would tell you "Everyone wanted to come and see Shelly"! When once asked "what do you want to do when you grow up" Shelly simply smiled and shouted "EVERYTHING"! – Now I was recently reminded that later she did focus her career aspirations down a bit to simply...you guessed it "A ROCK STAR"!

It was during these brief snapshots of time with Shelly that I was able to fully appreciate some of her most endearing qualities: her incredible bravery, unquenchable spirit for life, and unblemished love for her Nana, Papa and mom. I firmly believe that these attributes are a direct reflection of the love and support she always felt from each and every one of you.

Over the last several months I have often reflected on Shelly's life and wondered how she was able to approach so many challenges with such courage....

1. her incredibly resilient cancer
2. the nagging effects of steroids, radiation and chemotherapy and the
3. ultimate realization that her own death was eminent.

I believe that I have found the answer, at least in part, in one of my favorite passages of Scripture. In 2Corinthians 12:7-12, St. Paul confesses: To keep me from becoming conceited, there was given me a thorn in my flesh to torment me, (perhaps in Shelly's case her Neuroblastoma). Three times I pleaded with the Lord to take it away. But he said to me, brother, My grace is sufficient for you, for my power is made perfect in weakness. Therefore St Paul continues, I will boast all the more gladly about my weaknesses, so that Christ's power may rest on me. That is why I delight in weakness, in hardships, in difficulties and in suffering, for when I am weak, then I am strong.

Friends, I am here today to provide testimony that from Shelly's weakness and untimely death, has emerged incredible strength. In Shelly... a level of courage and resilience that truly superseded any human ability and enabled her to endure the consequences of a prolonged illness. In Jim, Bonnie and Ajay: incredible grace, fortitude and determination. I will never forget when Bonnie told me how she prayed that our Lord would "take Shelly's tumor and give it to her" only to later be diagnosed with lung cancer herself.... Jim and Ajay, my respect for both of you as individuals and as a devoted mother and papa reached new heights following Bonnie's passing; you never wavered in caring for Shelly and I trust you will find comfort in knowing that you confidently and courageously made all of the right decisions every step of the way.

And finally in me and in all of my colleagues....an incredible sense of our sadness and heart-felt emotions all to appropriate for this occasion as after an incredible struggle against an unrelenting disease, we lay our dear Shelly to rest to be at peace with our Lord. But rather to simply mourn Shelly's untimely death, it is clear that we are gathered to celebrate the years that we were blessed with her amazing presence. Shelly's life was characterized by unconditional love, undaunted bravery and immeasurable joy. To all of you here today, please never forget this...Let Shelly's spirit live inside of you and support you in your own times of grief, sadness or hardship.

As we rejoice knowing that Shelly is finally free of pain and suffering, where in the loving arms of her dear Nana each day includes a Disney cruise, all the lobster and ice cream a kid can eat and shopping for toys 24/7!..., we must still struggle with the selfish desire to have her back in our presence.

Jim and Ajay, thank you for letting me and my colleagues be a part of your lives and for giving all of us the opportunity to do God's work on this earth. Caring for Shelly has been nothing short of a privilege for me, but getting to know her and your family has been a true blessing. Jim, please know how much I admire you. You are one of the most kind and caring individuals I know, and through your love and devotion to your family, faith in God, and perseverance through life's most difficult trials, you have brought much comfort to me and have affirmed a rich, personal meaning to Philippians 4:13 "We can do all things through him who gives us strength"

Please always know that our team did everything in their power to cure Shelly of her relentless disease. May God bless you and strengthen you during this difficult time.

Good bye Shelly, you will be so dearly missed....never forgotten..... and forever loved as your spirit for life remains in the hearts of those you have left behind.

With adoration, respect and love...Dr. Ken

I wondered who would, or could follow Dr. Cooke's testimony. The next speaker nailed it. Nicholas, Shelly's boyfriend (the one she kissed on the second day of Kindergarten on the bus) marched up and professed his love and pain for Shelly. Other stories were very overwhelming for me, and I'll cherish each and every one of them. Ava, a five year old cancer victim, and new friend of Shelly's told of her love and inspiration she received from Shelly. Camp Quality Direct Kerri Fabios talked about how inspiring Shelly was to other campers, how she got so much out of life, and how she will be terribly missed. And Kelly Doyle, Shelly's camp companion for three years, talked about how much fun Shelly and she had at camp, and that she will be truly missed.

As with all church services, and funeral protocol, cell phones are requested to be turned off. I, not wanting to leave my phone in my coat pocket, asked my older daughter, Elaine, to put mine in her purse, which she did. Knowing that I get very few calls, and anybody that calls me would be at the funeral, I forgot to turn mine off (I had other things on my mind). During Chaplain Mike's reading, low and behold it went off. I recognized the ring tone immediately, and didn't move. Elaine finally figured it out, and by the time she got to it, it had stopped ringing. At the meal after, we relayed the fau pas to Mike, and he told us he observed a number of people in the audience reaching for their phone to see if it was theirs. It was over, we would mourn, and eventually find peace.

A number of people made contributions to help with the funeral cost. Although I cannot list them all, I would be remiss if I didn't mention major contributions by Hugs N Bugs, and Rev. Carol (Harrison) Barrett.

THE DAY AFTER

As we sat, not knowing what to do, how to go on, not really hungry, although many, many people brought food for us, Ajay received a phone call from Cousin Rick. There were a lot of police cars up the street at Steve's house. Steve was being arrested, again. He had been back manufacturing Crystal Meth, and the police raided his home and gathered evidence. Living within 200 feet of a school, he was facing a second felony charge of possession, manufacturing, and who knew what else. Boy, could things get any worse?

Well, the answer to that was YES. Two days later, while Steve was in jail, somebody torched his house, and it burned to the ground. Needless to say, he had let his insurance expire. The good times just keep on rolling.

After going his bail a month later, he was under house arrest, and on August 1 he accepted a 'plea deal' and was sentenced to four years, minimum in the Ohio Penal system.

Ajay, along with her boyfriend, and I continue to try to hold it together and find some purpose to our lives. We have counseling regularly, and, at times, it's everything that we can do to just through the day.

I have been asked "Jim, do you wish the last six years were different?"

The obvious answer is "Of course!", but the gifts we as a family have received from this experience are insurmountable. I have met so many wonderful people, so many people that have reached out to my family with help, so many people that are good in the world that I would have probably never met. I feel that there is hope in the world, for the world, that I truly believe that God is with us and walks with us. There were the organizations that were there for us: Make A Wish, Give Kids the World, Wings of Flight, United Air Lines, Hugs N Bugs, Camp Quality Ohio, and The Stephen J. Cannale Foundation. There are so many people that have truly blessed our lives. From Dr. Cooke, Dr. Egler, Linda Cabral, Nurse Lucilla Mack, and the wonderful UH staff who fought with us every step of the way. From Rev. Carol Barrett, Chaplain Mike Garren, and Hospice Chaplains like Patti Kelleher and volunteers like Charlie Loeffler, George Vasile and Bill (the book reader) Spalacy. And others, the families of cancer victims like Laura and Bill Ward, Christine Bradley and Luke, Lexie and Noah, Angela Konopinski and Emily, the Turner family, the Hostetlers, the Hostutlers, Shanda Louzander and Luke and Laura, Debbie Higgins and her family, the Magyars, the Lehmans, and so many more. For the supporting people, the Milos, Karan Ankney and family, the staff of Camp Quality, Kerri Fabios, Carol Cross, Tom Quinn, Ann Kagarise, companions Abby, Karla, Kelly, and others, like Lisa Stadvec and MaryBeth. Wonderful support people from Palliative care, Dr. Lisa Humphrey, Helen Gutin, Dr. Yip, Nurse Angie and many more. People that opened their hearts to Shelly, Gymnastic instructor Amy Alexander, neighbor Polly Bowman, and the whole school staff: Kati Kawza, Beth Harington, Ann Rochford, Mrs. McLean, Mrs. Brutz and her husband John, Mrs. Birdwise, John Vantrease. Park friends Belinda Thomas and her kids, Kara and Jared. Individuals like Susie and Ralph Hanes, Shirley and Jon Swires, Carole Kurilko, our maid of honor, Vaughn Gofney for Ajay, and more. Family: Terry and Geri Thornton, Grandma Thornton, Elaine and Bob Wallace, Steve Wallace and his wife Sally, and of course Cousin Rick Phillips. Most of these people we would have never known if it wasn't for Shelly, and we have been truly blessed by knowing them. I feel the world is in better shape than I had thought, thinking that most people don't care about their neighbor. Once again I was wrong.

The most important person I am thankful for is Shelly. This amazing little girl looked Cancer in the eye and said "I won't back down! I'm far from throwing in the towel. I have a whole lot of living to do, and I'm going to spread joy and love to everyone that I meet. I'm going to make them laugh, make them cry, but most of all, show them how to appreciate and to help one another. I'm going to do things on my bucket list, and don't you forget it. I will walk with Jesus and Nana in Heaven, and you can't stop me!"

If there is one message I would like you to take from 'Shelly's Song' it would be that you must be the advocate for your child, and their sickness. Ask questions, get second opinions, if the treatment isn't going well, find another treatment. I know, it's easy to say, but when dealing with a terminal illness, it can be overwhelming. I know, Shelly passed, but I feel that I did all that I could to help. Sometimes, even with the Lord by your side, that's all you can do. When it's done, just lean on the Lord, because He wanted your loved one, and they will be waiting for you in Heaven. I know that when my death comes, I will see Bonnie and Shelly again. Boy, what a day, Glorious Day that will be.

Farewell my dear best friend, you and Nana will always be in my heart.

In closing, I ask you to pray for a cure for Cancer, which is taking our children from us.

Thank you and God Bless,
Jim

EPILOGUE

January, 2014, eleven months after Shelly passed

Ajay and her boyfriend, Fabio, had chosen to live in my basement. By doing odd jobs, usually cleaning out and refurbishing vacated apartments, they have accumulated a lot of junk (in my opinion). In fact, one person called it an ancient Indian trailer park burial ground (my apologies to all native Americans). I would not, nor wanted to go to the basement, wondering how I would ever get that mess cleaned up if I would choose to sell the house.

As part of my regular medical checkup, I had a colonoscopy scheduled (not one of my favorite things, but it is what it is). Ajay volunteered to take me, as long as we got back by noon so that she could take Fabio to a job interview. Since my appointment was at 8:30, and the procedure was supposedly no more than 2 hours long, I felt it would work. Well, a power outage in the building delayed my procedure until 11 o'clock. I told Ajay to go and take Fabio to the interview and then come back for me.

On Ajay's way home she got a frantic call from Fabio saying that he burned himself and caught the house on fire. The fire started in their microwave, which sat on a dresser inside the bedroom door (in the basement). He had put the fire out, but burned himself badly in doing so. As she was almost home, she told him that she could get him to the ER faster that calling the squad, which she did so. Because of the severity of the burns, she called Cousin Rick to come and get me. She told us that she was on her way to the hospital, as the local ER life-flighted him to the burn unit in Akron.

When I got home, the fire was out, with a little residual smoke smell. I surveyed the damage, and decided that it was significant enough to call my homeowners insurance company. The adjuster agreed to come out two days later, a Saturday, and assess the damage, which he did. He felt that it was a minor claim, less than $25000 (MINOR! WOW). He said that he would send some contractors out the following Tuesday to do a more thorough evaluation. Ajay in the meantime was staying at the hospital with Fabio, who was in an induced coma to deal with the smoke damage to his lungs.

On Tuesday the contractors arrived and walked through the entire house. One of them had a white sponge that he would use the swipe on wall surfaces to determine the presence of smoke damage. The results showed that there was smoke damage throughout the house. Ajay happened to show up at that time and asked a few questions before they left.

No sooner had they departed than there was a knock on the door. (Don't people see my two doorbell buzzers?) I opened the door and there was a policeman and a detective, who asked if they may come in. I replied "Sure, what may I do for you?"

"I heard you had a fire here, but you didn't call us or the fire department" the detective said.

"That's right. By the time I got home the fire was out, and I called my insurance company. I didn't know I had to call you or the fire department."

Meanwhile Ajay was standing there. "May I see the fire damage?" replied the detective.

"Right this way" and I led him down the stairs to the damaged area. I chose not to stay down there with him, and returned upstairs. Ajay requested to leave, and was told by the patrolman that she must wait. The detective returned and stated that there was evidence of drug manufacturing downstairs, and wanted permission to do a more thorough search, stating he could get a search warrant in 2 to 3 hours, as there was probable cause.

I had nothing to hide, so I told him "Sure, go ahead".

Ajay requested to leave again, and was told that she cannot leave at this time. Within 30 minutes, the county Hazmat team showed up along with the county drug unit and two more squad cars. To further fill my cul-de-sac, two fire squads came where Ajay announced that she was two months pregnant. After being checked out by the ER units, Ajay and I were sitting on the couch and the detective approached us. "Someone has been manufacturing crystal methaphetamine in the basement, and I will be making an arrest.

So who do I arrest?" My mind was still struggling with the fact that there was drug manufacturing in my basement.

Ajay spoke up "Arrest me, my father doesn't know anything about it" As she was being led away, she said to me "Dad, I knew nothing about it, and the fire was started by grease on french fries that Fabio had put in the microwave. Please believe me."

"Ajay, if you want me to say I believe you, OK, I will. But the fact remains that you will have to convince the judge and jury, not me."

I asked the detective if the insurance company contacted him, and he said "No, it was the hospital, crystal meth was found in Fabio's blood."

Ajay got carted off to jail, with a court date set two days later. Since Fabio was in a coma in the hospital, no warrant was issued for him. The county did not want responsibility for transporting him daily for medical treatment after he came out of the drug induced coma. At the court, bailed was set at $25000, cash. I said "Have a nice day" and two week later, when the bail went to 10%, I said "have a nice day" and meant it.

In the meantime, Fabio was released from the hospital, and no one knew it. He was dropped off at Cousin Rick's house. Fabio and Ajay were friends with Rick, and had done some work for him. Two weeks later when Ajay's bail was reduced to a signature bond her lawyer asked where she would go. Since the insurance company had removed me from my premises and put me an Extended Stay motel nearby, she could not stay at home or with me, so she said she would stay with Cousin Rick.

I commented "Fabio's staying there, and the police still haven't picked him up yet". Ajay's lawyer said that they could not stay at the same place and Ajay should not make contact with him, so a call was made to Rick who told Fabio he would have to leave. I also called the police again and told them Fabio's location. Fabio left and the police showed up 2 hours later. Fabio was on the streets. Ajay's court date was near the end of April, so she settled in at Rick's.

Because the fire was as a result of illegal drug activity, the insurance company would not fix any damage caused by the Meth. But they would repair/replace anything that was either smoke or fire damage (Yea, I'm still confused). The plan was to get an environmental evaluation to determine the limit of contamination. The insurance company would not pay for that, so I had to shell out over $1000 to have it done. The results showed that (from just 4 samples) everything in the basement was contaminated, and must be thrown out. The upstairs was only smoke damage. The extra cost of the cleaning people wearing disposable coverings would be to my expense. The plan was to remove everything from the top two floors after sealing the basement door. Once that was done, a plastic tunnel was made from the basement door to the front door, to prevent any cross-contamination when emptying the basement. After the basement was emptied, filling 4 dumpsters, then the cleanup and rehab could be done.

During this time I decided to have back surgery, having a herniated disc causing severe pain as I tried to take frequent walks. On rehab, while watching TV, Ajay enters and says "I was just at the baby doctor, and he told me when the baby was due".

"When was that?", eager to find out myself.

"Next October" she replied.

"Wait a minute, you said in January you were 2 months pregnant, that doesn't add up, you sure that's what the doctor told you?" sensing that she knew she'd been caught in another lie.

"Yea" she replied "I told him that didn't seem right"

That conversation occurred in late April. Two days later I get a call from Ajay "Dad, I'm in the hospital, I had a heart attack".

Still skeptical, knowing she loves to play the sympathy card I ask "Which hospital?" To which she replied the Lakewood Hospital (west of Cleveland). "What are you doing in Lakewood?"

"We came up here to get tires for my car." This just continues to get more and more ridiculous. Don't they have tires in Akron anymore? Lord help me.

Still skeptical, I ask "How did you get there?"

"Oh, Cousin Rick brought me". I requested to speak to Rick to verify this outrageous story, and she said he had went to get a cup of coffee. Figures.

To my surprise, Rick called me back and verified the whole story.

Over the next few weeks, Rick and I alternately visited Ajay in the hospital. She was in ICU because of the blockage in her left ventricle required a shunt, and they had a hard time stabilizing her, so they induced a coma as she was very combative. While visiting her I stumbled into Fabio, who was visiting her. He quickly left the hospital. Talking to Rick afterward I found out that he was staying with a friend in Lakewood. I called the Copley with this information and they said they would notify the local police.

After she was brought out of the induced coma, Ajay fell and hit her head, causing internal bleeding, so a drain was placed in her head. She was one sick person. The hospital decided that she would get better care being transferred to the Cleveland Clinic. Once again I contacted the Copley with this information, and it was forwarded to the Clinic Police department.

Ajay, upon entering the Lakewood hospital, had given Fabio as the primary person to contact, with Rick as backup. The Clinic police contacted Fabio and said they needed his signature to perform a procedure on Ajay, so, when he showed up, he was immediately arrested.

The next morning Rick notified me of the arrest. I asked where her car was, assuming it was still at his place, because that's where I thought it was where he took her to Lakewood to buy tires and she had her heart attack. He said no, it was in Lakewood, and he was going to take her there with the tires. Then he said that Fabio had been driving it. This really irritated me, as I had been making payments on the car and insurance. I asked where is it now? He replied that it was probably at the Cleveland Clinic. Wonderful.

The next day when I went to visit Ajay, I decided to search for her car. Although the Cleveland Clinic has over 5000 employees, and numerous parking lots, I figured he would have parked her car close to the entrance that he would use to visit Ajay. Bingo! I couldn't believe it. There it was, about 15 cars up the ramp from the entrance. Wow! How was I sure it was her car? It was unlocked, with a window down. In the backseat was her purse (empty, of course). I wasn't that lucky, there were no keys in it.

I contacted Rick and he went to the Akron Jail to get the keys from Fabio's belongings, and the next day we drove up to get her car.

I cautioned him not to leave me, feeling the car still needed a tire, or maybe out of gas. Neither was the case. I drove it home, and was fuming that Fabio was driving her car, without a license, and I was making payments and paying her insurance. Yes, I know, how dumb can a person be? I guess I found out.

Ajay was released a few days later and stayed with Rick until her sentencing date. They offered her a plea deal, 30 months mandatory, and she took it. Sentencing was to be the end of August.

She took her car, and drove it occasionally. I found out that we, I, was upside down on the car's financing. I owed more than it was worth. Great. The good times just keep on coming. I contacted my nephew, Jon, who is the manager of a Chevy dealership in Massillon to see if he could get me out of this mess, and he replied that they do it all the time. I gave Ajay what the car was worth, and traded her vehicle and mine in and purchased an Impala. I told her that she's on her own. I will not help her financially anymore. She understood, and bought an old 'beater' to drive, and used the rest of the money to bail Fabio our of jail.

Fabio got sentenced on August 28 to 3 years mandatory plus 8 months for parole violation. Ajay was sentenced on September 2 to 30 months mandatory.